adult literacy education in the united states

Wanda Dauksza Cook

International Reading Association
800 Barksdale Road • Newark, Delaware 19711

Copyright 1977 by the
International Reading Association, Inc.

Library of Congress Cataloging in Publication Data

Cook, Wanda D.
    Adult literacy education in the United States.

    Bibliography: p.
    1. Adult education—United States. 2. Illiteracy—
United States. I. Title.
LC5251.C63   374'.012'0973   76-58957
ISBN 0-87207-934-1

Contents

Foreword

It is most appropriate that, following America's Bicentennial year, the International Reading Association publish this scholarly account of the country's achievements in the area of adult literacy education. In many ways, Dr. Cook's historical study reveals both strengths and weaknesses of the nation's character, economy, and past and present educational priorities.

Adult Literacy Education in the United States stresses the problems, accomplishments, and failures of American adult literacy education from 1900 until the present decade. As the reader moves through the volume, she/he will become aware of the changing social philosophy and its effect on education in general and literacy education in particular. Of particular interest to some readers will be the period from 1960 to the present time. During this period, Americans became acutely aware of the plight of native born functional illiterates and educators recognized that literacy education, offered in isolation from economic and other social problems, was relatively ineffective. This awareness brought about the present period of experimentation and the search for multiple causalities and solutions to the literacy problem which is now regarded as both social and educational.

Recently, a national survey revealed that approximately 25 percent of our adult population is severely handicapped in dealing with such skills as reading and mathematics and such areas of information as occupational knowledge, consumer economics, health, and government and law. Unlike many of the functional illiterates of fifty to one hundred years ago, most of this population has attended public schools for six or more years; many are high school graduates. It is now obvious that new solutions must be sought to this continuing problem. All too often in the past (often due to a lack of knowledge of our literacy history) old solutions were rediscovered and reapplied, and the problem persisted. This historical study may aid us in avoiding past mistakes and help us in the search for better solutions.

Adult Literacy Education in the United States will prove useful to educators in general, persons doing research in the area of reading, and administrators and teachers who are seeking new and better ways of meeting the problems of undereducated adolescents and adults. It will also prove useful to librarians and that host of generous and concerned volunteer workers who are dedicated to bringing about a better life for the less advantaged population.

Dr. Cook's historical study reveals the heretofore crisis approach to adult literacy education in America. Over the years, in times of crisis, the main body of Americans kept rediscovering the literacy problems and, over the years, hastily contrived solutions to the problem were invented or reinvented. As the crisis passed, so did the concern of America's leaders; now we are in a different time and in a different social climate. No longer are leaders looking for simple and fast solutions to the problem; its complexity is well recognized. Organizations such as the International Reading Association, the Adult Education Association of America, Churchwomen United, and the National Association for Public School and Continuing Adult Education are accepting the responsibility for aiding in solving the long term problem of meeting the educational needs of undereducated adults. The United States Office of Education and the various state departments of education are committed to the development of better programs for undereducated adults. Dr. Cook's study will aid them in preventing the recurrence of errors committed in the past and in the development of future programs. A profession that does not know where it has been is unlikely to know where it is going.

Edwin H. Smith
Florida State University

Acknowledgements

It is my pleasant task to express my deep appreciation to those who have encouraged and helped me to complete this book. I am grateful to the staffs of the Government Documents Division and the Interlibrary Loan Department of the University of Massachusetts Library for their cooperation in locating materials for me. I would also like to thank the staff members of the Center for Applied Linguistics in Washington, D.C. for the use of their files and for other kindnesses.

I particularly want to thank Rita Warner for her part in the preparation of the manuscript. Her friendship and nimble fingers preserved my mental health. Finally, I would like to thank the International Reading Association for accepting this book for publication, the reviewers for their helpful suggestions and comments, and Faye Branca for her assistance in the preparation of the final manuscript.

WDC

Introduction

The problem of illiteracy is one which is basic to all countries, whether they are prosperous, emerging or underdeveloped. It is true that, in recent years, illiteracy figures have shown steady improvement; but it is only during this past decade that the true burden of illiteracy has been realized.

The ultimate demands made of man in growing and changing societies show progress to be inadequate in many instances. Without basic literacy skills, countless people are forced to live their lives in poverty. Often they are without adequate housing, food, or health care and are unable to participate fully in society. Furthermore, many leave illiteracy as a legacy for their children.

If a society learns and grows from what has gone before, a history of literacy education should provide some direction in attacking this problem. Although histories of education are prevalent, no previous single source provides an overview of the history of American literacy education. The records of past successes and failures have remained scattered and few communities, states, or countries have been able to learn from these early endeavors. This history shares that knowledge.

Other countries may find this study useful as a model for similar investigations. The translation of such histories into other languages would permit a worldwide picture of the problems and solutions encountered in adult literacy education.

Here, then, is an attempt to set forth the various phases through which American literacy education has passed. The reader will note that the federal government's concern with the problem surfaces mainly during times of national conflict. The history is one which is characterized by individual efforts implemented by state and local governments. The reader's attention is focused primarily on the legislation, programs, and methods and materials which have resulted from these independent actions.

Each time one brings new information from the past into the present, history is brought into sharper focus. It is even more appropriate during America's Bicentennial year to reflect upon the past, for knowing where we have been will give direction for the future.

WDC

Chapter One

1900-1909: Americanization and Literacy Education

Social Climate

Attitudes

Movements and events leading to the twentieth century placed the United States in a position to become increasingly concerned with the educational development of its people. Prior to 1900, the United States directed its attention toward expansion of the western frontiers, development of communication and transportation systems, and industrialization. Once these goals were reached, interests shifted to the social problems of the nation.

The movement west was undertaken with such zeal that only basic skills for survival were considered important. Since the settlers were able to function with a high degree of efficiency, their lack of education did not appear to be a matter of great import. Reading and writing, though obviously not a hindrance, were not regarded as vital skills and few efforts were made to educate the many illiterate adults who settled the frontier.

Once the western boundaries of the nation were reached, concern shifted realistically to connecting the eastern seaboard with the western settlements. The most monumental undertaking in this direction was construction of the transcontinental railroad. For reasons of economy and efficiency, developers exploited the availability of Asian immigrants to supply inexpensive, unskilled labor needed to accomplish the task.

Little thought was given to the social or economic implications which might result from the influx of a large group of persons so obviously different from native born Americans in appearance, customs, and language. A large illiterate group, able and willing to subsist on meager wages and live under poor conditions, presented a threat to working persons in the West. This threat, combined with prejudices created by language and color barriers, fostered discrimination laws which by 1882 prohibited further immigration of Chinese (*28:* 475). Such laws prohibited further immigration but made no provision for assimilating the thousands of Orientals who had already migrated. This problem was not yet recognized.

The Easterner experienced similar prejudices in coping with the new immigrants arriving from eastern and southern Europe who also were willing to work for low wages. Groups settled together in ethnic neighborhoods that often deteriorated into ghettos and thus helped spread suspicion among native born Americans.

The struggle between old and new immigrants eventually led to the formation of groups such as the Immigration Restriction League, which proposed the use of literacy tests to restrict immigration in the hope that such tests would eliminate the migration of persons from eastern and southern parts of Europe. Henry Cabot Lodge became an active leader in the cause.

> According to a bill he proposed in 1896, only those who could read and write their own or some other language might be admitted. The test, he stated frankly, would "bear most heavily upon the Italians, Russians, Poles, Hungarians, Greeks and Asiatics, and very lightly, or not at all, upon English-speaking immigrants or Germans, Scandinavians and French." In his opinion, "the mental and moral qualities which make what we call our race" could be preserved only by excluding "the wholesale infusion of races whose traditions and inheritances, whose thoughts and beliefs are wholly alien to ours and with whom we have never assimilated or even been associated in the past" (*28:* 475).

This bill and similar efforts made in 1909 and 1915 were passed in Congress but were vetoed by the incumbent presidents.

The growth of illiteracy was also nurtured by two prevailing attitudes of the general public: 1) the belief that the United States is a country where no one is *compelled* to do anything hindered enforcement of school attendance laws designed to prevent illiteracy, and 2) the people were not willing to submit to intervention in education. Their philosophy was that "they would rather take the chances of a great peril, in the belief that if the chance went against them their resourcefulness would be able to cure the difficulty when the time came" (*212:* 539).

Motivations

With such negative attitudes prevailing during this period, what was it that motivated the few efforts directed toward literacy education? The answer might well have been the desire to assimilate the foreigners. The process of learning a new language, new customs, and the fundamentals of American democracy was slow and tedious since the majority of persons entering the country were classified as illiterate. In this instance, "illiterates [were] those who [had] not learned to write in any language" (252: 5).

Viewing the problem of illiteracy during the beginning of the twentieth century, Talbot stressed the fact that literacy was a first requisite for democracy. "Unless means are provided for reaching the illiterate and near illiterate, every social problem must remain needlessly complex and slow in solution, because social and representative government rests upon an implied basis of universal ability to read and write" (252: 5). The growing number of both foreign born and native born illiterates made this problem even more apparent.

The Statistics

The 1900 census defined an illiterate as any person ten years of age or older who was unable to read and write his native language. The literacy question was phrased so the individual was able to answer with a "yes" or "no" (271: xcvii). The census revealed that 6,180,069 persons answered "no" to the literacy question. Approximately 10.7 percent of the population in the United States was classified as illiterate in 1900.

Examination of the figures revealed that 51.8 percent of the illiterates were Caucasian while the remaining 48.2 percent were Negro, Chinese, Indian, and other nonwhite groups. The census confirmed the fact that foreign born whites were arriving from the less educated countries and their arrival added to America's illiteracy problem. In 1900, 20.8 percent of the illiterate population were foreign born white, as compared with 18.1 percent in 1890. This indicated a sizeable increase during the decade (271: xciv).

One might reasonably expect that the numbers of foreign-born whites unable to function in their environments were even greater than reported. An individual capable of communicating in his native tongue still could find the language barrier a great obstacle.

A sectional breakdown of the census revealed that particular groups of illiterates existed. The majority of illiterates in the North Atlantic states were foreign born whites; in the North Central states, Indian; in the South Atlantic and South Central states, blacks; and in the Western states, native whites with Spanish speaking parents and Indians (271: cxii).

Whether native or foreign born, these illiterates were examples of wasted economic and human potential.

Programs

Although illiteracy was not yet recognized during this period as a national social problem, there were specific interest groups which viewed illiteracy as a serious matter. Each group established its own program to bridge the wide gap of illiteracy; each was prompted by its own motives.

Labor union programs

In his account of the history of the International Ladies Garment Workers Union, Louis Levine cited an early labor effort to educate illiterates. "In November 1890, a Cloak Maker's Social Educational Club was organized in New York to teach members of the Cloak Maker's Union how to read and write English and how to become citizens" (*38*: 483). The author further noted that

> ...these early efforts were necessarily sporadic and undifferentiated in purpose. No line was drawn between education, propaganda, politics and revolutionary agitation. The socialists taught the cloak-makers at the same time how to read and write and how to sign the cross in the socialist column of the ballot.

The rapid growth of local unions made it necessary to have informed and educated members. To promote this end, several international locals in New York arranged to use the public schools for lectures, courses, and shop meetings. "For several years it remained the only labor union in America carrying on such activities" (*38*: 496).

Management views

The necessity for literacy education was demonstrated in many areas of industry. As Mrs. Fred Bagley reported to the House Committee on Education:

> The Director of the Bureau of Mines states that the removal of illiteracy among miners, who are mostly foreigners, would save annually 1,000 lives and 150,000 injuries. One-half of all industrial accidents are due to inability to understand danger warnings. True economy certainly would suggest that a step forward in the banishment of illiteracy is of the greatest importance (*217*: 15).

Examining the industrial problem, Talbot made the following concrete suggestion and, in so doing, placed some of the responsibility on the shoulders of industry.

4

Effective measures to reduce adult illiteracy can become possible by closer cooperation between industry and education. Industry can make it possible by allowance of time and wage to enable illiterate adult workers—who can earn usually but small wages, often because of their illiteracy and things that go with illiteracy—to learn to read and write, and in a minimum time of 60 hours enable them to surmount their worst obstacles to progress. The public schools can provide teachers. Illiterate workers are expensive workers. There seems to be no more effective, practical, and economical way of meeting the problem of the unemployed adult illiterate than by means of the workers' public-school day class. By its adoption, much industrial inefficiency and social waste may rapidly be eliminated (252: 16).

Even then, the untrained worker was unable to compete effectively with his literate counterpart. Schooling could help the worker realize the reasons for his low and unstable wages, aid in removing the suspicions and prejudices that accompany the alien, and help reduce the waste of industry.

Community efforts

An example of a community effort to deal with foreign born illiterates took place in Passaic, New Jersey, a textile town of approximately 60,000 people. An investigation revealed that "in 1910 one out of every three people 10 years of age and over in Passaic could not speak English; 55 percent of all the foreign born 10 years of age and over could not speak English" (264: 7).

Each year, only about 250 adults were being taught to read and write through evening schools, although many more adults were registered. The following reasons for low attendance keep reappearing as major factors to be considered when planning programs for illiterate adults.

1. Working days or nights produced a conflict with classes, mothers were not able to leave their homes, and men could not find the energy to study after a long workday.

2. There were communication barriers between students and teachers. Programs had been organized utilizing the teachers available with little concern given to the previous training of the teachers. In fact, the importance of having teachers specifically trained for teaching adults was not yet fully realized. This did not become an area of concern until some years later.

3. Too often, the methods employed by teachers offended adults. Childish sentences, dull topics, and choral recitations did not allow for individual progress and, on the whole, these unsophisticated methods discouraged two-thirds of the students.

The completed investigation produced a list of suggestions which the New Jersey Bureau of Education felt would help with the problem.

1. It recommended that a separate Department of Adult Education be established and the department would function with a complete staff of its own. Aiding this organization would be an advisory council composed of representatives from clubs, nationality groups, and labor.
2. It advised that courses be designed using teachers of different nationalities. Each teacher would instruct his own nationality group.
3. It was also suggested a native born and a foreign born teacher should share a class.
4. It was recommended that day courses be offered in the late afternoon hours to accommodate workers. All such classes would be grouped to provide better instruction.
5. Finally, industries should be encouraged to provide time for study without loss of wages (264: 24).

Legislation

While these attempts to deal with adult illiteracy were taking place, some states were attempting to deal with the same problem in another manner. They aimed at preventing illiteracy by concentrating their efforts on training the children.

New York State

In 1906, the Commission of Education in New York State investigated the problem of illiteracy. The investigation revealed that illiteracy existed in both the rural and urban areas of the state, and that it rapidly decreased among the children of foreign born parents. Finally, the study showed that the general attitudes of the citizens were negative and did not encourage literacy.

To help remedy the situation, the commission suggested that more emphasis be placed on mandatory school attendance. Although New York had had a compulsory attendance law since 1854, the law had not been enforced. Penalties aimed at parents and children were designed to provide teeth for the law (212: 551).

To supplement the law and help eliminate the roots of illiteracy, child labor legislation was provided. It prohibited children under age fourteen from working in factories and those between fourteen and sixteen were required to have certificates (212: 551). Further restrictions were placed on the number of hours of work and the type of employment in which a youth could participate. Basically, then, New York attempted to reduce adult illiteracy before it began by legally placing children in school.

6

Virginia

The problem of illiteracy was not confined to the foreign born and to the industrial areas of the North. The less urban and rural areas of the South suffered a similar problem with native born citizens. Here, too, the efforts to remedy the situation were sporadic.

Virginia also directed its endeavors toward the prevention of illiteracy. In 1908, a statute was enacted placing a compulsory school law on the books *(279:* 16). However, it contained an option which left it within the power of a school district to avail itself of the law if it cared to do so. It was hardly what one would call a strong statute. Yet, those districts following it claimed they met with satisfactory results.

In an attempt to deal with illiteracy at the adult level, the Richmond School Board exerted a great effort toward establishing adult evening schools. Studies included subjects from grade level one through high school and were available to anyone over age fourteen.

Since people moved about freely during this time, the efforts of individual states did not prove adequate in making a significant contribution to the reduction of illiteracy. A certain uniformity among the states was needed. As a result, some states were particularly eager to have the federal government become active with legislation which would prohibit persons over fourteen from entering the country unless they were able to read and write in some language *(212:* 557). They felt that this action would help, in part, to alleviate the problem of illiteracy.

Methods and Materials

Materials

Very little appears to have been done in the area of curriculum materials during the first decade of the century. Existing materials were directed toward the teaching of the foreign born and not the native born illiterate.

During this period, most of the bibliographies were designed for expanding teacher background concerning the foreign born. Butler included a fairly extensive list in his publication, *Community Americanization (256:* 77-82). He included books on the immigrant mind, background of races, and teaching a language.

Teaching English to Aliens (268) was a fairly extensive bibliography which referenced many curriculum texts used during the decade. Instructional books for the illiterate were few in number and not particularly varied in design. For the most part, a reading selection was presented and then followed by a series of questions related to the passage. The questions might utilize conversation, word drill, or sentence drill. Few, if any, reading skills were taught. English and civics texts were most commonly used for instructional purposes but, occasionally, recreational books were used as supplements. Quite often these supplements were children's reading texts.

Methods

The instructional methods used with adults were not particularly sophisticated during the initial portion of this century. One approach tried was the synthetic method. Based primarily on grinding drill, this building method proved to be unnatural as it progressed from alphabet to words to phrases and sentences.

Teachers often made use of the direct method of teaching. The premise of this technique was the more reading matter a student hears, the sooner he will be able to use it. Although the basic idea was good, its execution was often poor. The choral recitations usually produced memorized passages accompanied by very little understanding.

It appears the most effective technique employed was the analytic method. Here the student started with a larger unit—the theme—which was composed of several short, related sentences. The selection, which was based on some useful topic and was fairly short in length, was then studied in terms of its components. Since these themes were often prepared by the teacher, it was not uncommon to supplement the lessons with commercial materials (*269*: 14-15).

Summary

The first decade of the twentieth century was characterized by heavy immigration. New immigrants were met with suspicion, prejudice, and disdain by native born Americans and "old immigrants." Since the new immigrants were mainly from less uniformly educated countries, they added to the already sizeable illiteracy problem in the United States.

The public generally displayed a lack of concern about illiteracy. The few attempts at literacy education were directed mainly at the immigrant segment of the population and the motivation for these classes was often less than noble.

Lack of uniform legislation and the mobility of the people hindered the few local efforts to educate the illiterate adult. Some states, such as New York, aimed at preventing adult illiteracy by placing the emphasis on educating the child.

One of the few attempts to study the problem of illiteracy took place in Passaic, New Jersey. The study resulted in a list of suggestions to the State Department of Education. In the years to follow, these results would be rediscovered many times over, but it would be many years before anything significant would be done about the problem.

And so with a few isolated comments and efforts, the history of adult literacy education started its evolution.

Chapter Two
1910-1919: Concern for the Native Born Illiterate

Social Climate

The spirit of reform

The first portion of the period from 1910 to 1919 found a progressive reform movement well under way. During the prosperous years before World War I, a spirit of reform flourished and affected almost every aspect of American life. The rise of women as a power in social and moral questions probably accounted, in part, for this prevailing mood.

The movement continued until about 1916. Reform was not only social, economic, and political but also extended to education. Federal grants to aid education were initiated in the Smith-Lever and Smith-Hughes acts. Talks began about establishing a Department of Education and state and local attempts at literacy education increased. With all these changes, the people were cautious not to let the federal government obtain too much power. Experiences with the rise of big businesses after the Civil War had made the people skeptical; and, as a result, reform was tempered with reserve.

Attitudes of prejudice, fear, and shock

By 1917, the United States was taking an active part in the European conflict. As a result, two distinct attitudes emerged in this country; and both had a direct bearing on literacy education. The first was a strong antiforeign born sentiment. The intense fear experienced by the people was evident in the statements made at the time.

At an education conference, Senator Lafayette Young of Iowa expressed his views: "I believe that 90 percent of all the men and women who teach the German language are traitors and out of sympathy with our government" (*253*: 35).

Richard Metcalf, of the Council of Defense of Nebraska, gave his opinion: "We have reached the conclusion that it is absolutely necessary to have a law that will bar from all grade schools, private as well as public, all foreign languages" (*253*: 38).

Despite attempts to shroud all that was foreign in influence, the fact remained that there was still a large foreign born population living in the United States. "We are 100 percent American in the state of Wyoming, and we are going to remain 100 percent American," said Governor Frank Houx (*253*: 59). The views he and others held provided the theme for a partial solution to the problem—Americanize the foreign element!

The entrance of the United States into World War I brought to the surface another problem of national proportion. Of all men tested for the draft, 25 percent were near-illiterate, that is, unable to read a newspaper intelligently or to write an intelligent letter (*64*: 633).

It was no uncommon thing during the late summer of 1917 for men to be arrested for their failure to register and brought before Federal officers. It was then disclosed that they were illiterate and did not know of the registration or draft, and some of them did not even know that the country was at war (*51*: 94).

For the first time, the federal government was deeply and justifiably concerned about the problem of adult illiteracy. Records indicated that out of the 10 million men in the first registration, approximately 700,000 were totally illiterate (*206*: 5).

And so, during the latter part of this period, literacy education had two distinct goals. The first goal, motivated by fear and suspicion, was to eliminate the foreign influence in this country through the process of Americanization. This automatically implied that oral and written English language had to be taught. The second goal was to help prepare some of the inductees for the service by providing them with the elements of reading and writing.

The Statistics

The results of the 1910 census revealed a drop in the illiteracy rate from 1900. In 1900, 10.7 percent of the population were counted as illiterate, while in 1910 only 7.7 percent were classified in this group (*238*: 1186).

The definition of illiterate used in 1910 varied slightly from the one used in 1900. In 1910, the census defined as illiterate any person ten years of age or older who was unable to write, regardless of ability to read. The individual did not have to be able to perform in English; any language was acceptable (*238*: 1185). In 1900, literacy required the person to be able to read *and* write in some language (*271*: xcvii).

Although there was a slight variation of definitions officially, in practical terms there was very little difference between the two. In 1910, there were a limited number of people who were able to read but could not write and, for general purposes, these numbers were often added to those who were officially illiterate. Those counted as literate often included people who were barely able to write their names or were able to read just a few words. Therefore, the figures of the census actually represented an estimate of illiterates rather than an absolute number.

Approximately 5,516,163 persons were counted as illiterate in this country in 1910. Of this group, 40.4 percent were Negro; 27.8 percent were native whites; 29.9 percent were foreign born whites; and the remaining 1.9 percent were Indian, Chinese, and other minority groups (*238*: 1186).

The number of illiterates in each of these groups dropped, with the exception of the foreign born whites. This segment of the illiterate population was still growing. In 1900, there were 1,287,135 illiterate foreign born persons in the United States. Ten years later, the number had increased to 1,650,361 (*238*: 1186).

Unfortunately, the general decline in illiteracy during the first decade of the century was not due to any effort exerted by federal, state, or local governments. Instead, the improvement was probably due to the improvements in educational opportunities. This idea is supported by the fact that in an age by age analysis, the older the group, the greater the illiteracy rate.

Legislation

The efforts exerted toward literacy education were still being conducted at a local level at the beginning of the decade. Stewart reported: "In 1910 there was not a law on the statute books of any of the states referring to adult illiteracy" (*51*: 163). One cannot help but notice that sporadic attempts to deal with the illiteracy problem did not generate enough concern to warrant even state laws.

The changing times

By the beginning of the second decade of the century, the spirit of reform had had its influence. In 1920, in some states, there were laws which provided for the organization of programs, the training of teachers, and the establishment of classes in mills.

In California, a literacy campaign was initiated in 1915 by the State Department of Education, the Immigration Commission, and the California Federation of Women's Clubs. Later that same year, the California "home teacher law" was passed. "The law provides an itinerant teacher to go from house to house and instruct illiterates and others" (51: 133).

Legislation and immigration

Another piece of legislation significant during this period was directed specifically toward the immigrant. The bill sought to use a literacy test to exclude certain groups of foreigners. Anyone sixteen years of age and over who could not read English or some other language would not be permitted to enter this country. Earlier efforts had been vetoed, but the fever of the war had made the people suspicious of foreigners and the 1917 attempt became law when Congress overrode President Wilson's veto (28: 625).

Programs

The moonlight schools of Kentucky

One of the best known and successful programs of this period concerned an attempt to deal with illiteracy in the rural areas of Kentucky. The program was initiated in Rowan County by Cora Wilson Stewart and might well be classified as the official beginning of literacy education in the United States.

As superintendent of public schools in Rowan County, Mrs. Stewart had firsthand contact with the problems experienced by the illiterate and decided to open the public schools to adults on moonlit nights. Thus, the now famous "moonlight schools" came into existence.

The schools opened on September 5, 1911 and were staffed by volunteer teachers. Twelve hundred adults arrived for instruction and virtually all were without previous schooling. Classes met four times a week, from seven to nine in the evening. The curriculum consisted of drills in basic language, history, civics, agriculture, and sanitation concepts (51: 14-18).

Since no texts were available, a small weekly newspaper was used for instructional purposes. *The Rowan County School Messenger*, edited by Mrs. Stewart, contained basically school and county news. It utilized short sentences and repetition of words for ease of reading with the first lesson using only eleven different words (51: 21):

Can we win?
Can we win what?
Can we win the prize?
Yes, we can win.
See us try.
And see us win!

To aid in writing instruction, the "moonlight school tablet" was used. The first page was a white sheet of blotting paper with the student's name indented on it. This was followed by colored sheets of blotting paper with indented letters, and the student traced them. The color provided interest and the grooves provided success.

By 1912, the movement had spread to twelve counties and the student enrollment rose to 1,600. During the summer of 1912, a teacher institute was held at Moorehead, Kentucky, for the purpose of training new volunteers for an expanded program.

"The experiment in Rowan County, Kentucky, shows that it is possible to bring help to illiterate men and women even under the most difficult and adverse circumstances" (*261*: 32). As a result of these efforts, Governor James McCreary established an illiteracy commission in Kentucky in 1914. This was the first illiteracy commission in the United States.

The true concern of the state, however, seems to be reflected in the fact that no appropriations were made to support the commission's work. The state supported the project in spirit only.

Other states launch campaigns

In 1913, Julia Selden initiated a movement in South Carolina and by 1918 state funds were being appropriated for an illiteracy commission.

Following the examples of Kentucky and South Carolina, Alabama waged its crusade in 1914. In only a year, the Alabama Illiteracy Commission was established, the second of its kind in the nation.

J. Joyner, State Superintendent of Public Instruction, organized the literacy campaign in North Carolina in 1914. By 1919, these schools became part of the public school system.

Moonlight schools were in operation in Oklahoma by 1914. M.E. Wood, a professor at the State Normal School in Edmond, and R.H. Wilson, State Superintendent of Education, were active in initiating the state's campaign. As part of the program, Oklahoma became the first state to have its Normal Schools offer credits for moonlight school work.

Several states became active participants in literacy campaigns in 1915. Washington enacted a law so school districts would be able to establish night schools. In Minnesota, literacy work was directed by the Naturalization Bureau. In New Mexico, the concept of the moonlight school found modification. Such schools were often filled with Mexican students who were learning English. Several laws were enacted which related to these schools. One noteworthy law provided compensation for those people teaching in a moonlight school with at least ten students (51: 131-132).

The literacy campaigns were not always accepted as eagerly as one might suspect in view of the seriousness of the problem. It was not unusual for the crusading advocates to be stopped by legislatures. The state of Georgia provides a good example of some of the prevailing attitudes.

As early as 1911, M.L. Brittain, State Supervisor of the Schools of Georgia, requested that the state legislature authorize workers and funds to be directed toward the eradication of illiteracy. These efforts met with no success since the legislators were firmly convinced that illiterate adults could not be taught with any degree of success. Unwilling to accept this, five school supervisors set up successful programs in their counties. With the success of the programs, a renewed effort was made. By 1919, eight years after its first appeal, Georgia established an illiteracy commission (51: 135).

Soon Mississippi, Arkansas, New York, Pennsylvania, and other states were following the examples set by Kentucky, North Carolina, and Georgia. The moonlight schools—whether they were called lay-by schools, schools for grown-ups, or community schools—appeared throughout the country as the movement spread. But it is perhaps wise to note that "an institution so new as a school where illiterate adults could learn to read and write may be misunderstood, criticized, and even resented by those who need it most" (51: 159). In many instances, this was exactly the case.

Industry and illiteracy

For the working adult, the chances of receiving or extending an elementary education were rare. Night schools, which were occasionally available, proved to be quite impractical in providing for the needs of factory workers. In most cases, classes were scheduled so late that the adult was too physically and mentally exhausted to take advantage of them.

A more efficient means of providing instruction was the "workers' class." In 1913 the New York City Workers' Class Experiment took place. Its purpose was to provide an elementary education for adults. The program involved the cooperation of public schools, industry, and the individual. The school system provided the teacher and equipment while the industrial establishment provided the room in the place of employment and the time for the students to attend class without loss of wages (*252:* 40-42).

In September 1913 the program was put into effect. Forty young women employed by the Dudley E. Sickler Company, maker of undergarments, were selected for instruction during the workday. Twenty workers received instruction from October to February and the remaining twenty from February to June. Each section was divided into groups of three or four girls and instruction was provided Monday through Friday for forty-five minutes a day. The curriculum was planned for its practical value as well as for academic merit.

Course of Study of the Illiterate Workers' Class (*252:* 46)

   I. English Language
     1. Reading
     2. Spelling
     3. Writing
     4. Geography
     5. Methods of Communication
       a. Correspondence
         Business letters
         Social letters
         Post office regulations
       b. Telephoning
       c. Telegraphing

  II. Hygiene
     1. Personal Cleanliness
     2. Physical culture (gymnastics)
     3. Food choice, food value, cooking, serving
     4. Emergencies—treatment of injured

 III. Civics
     1. Systems of government
       a. Merits of democratic governments
       b. Patriotism
       c. Citizenship
     2. History
       a. Origins of legal holidays
       b. Lives of statesmen

IV. Mathematics
1. Four fundamental operations in arithmetic
2. Tables of weights and measures
3. Money: bills and currency
4. Work reports
5. Personal expense accounts
6. Bank accounts

V. Practical Application of Language
1. Evolution of an undergarment
   a. Growth of cotton plant
   b. Manufacture
      Spinning operation
      Bleaching
   c. Weaving
   d. Shipping
2. Alphabet as a Guide to Common Things
   a. Advertisements
   b. Dictionary
   c. Directory

The curriculum content of the program was quite similar to that now recommended for modern adult basic education classes. The final report indicated the results were highly satisfactory. Students were enthusiastic, work efficiency improved 20-70 percent, and the hourly wage increased from 19.5¢ to 22.2¢ per hour. The nonclass group remained the same in efficiency and hourly wage (252: 47).

The General Chemical Works at Bayonne, New Jersey, instituted a class for workers in October 1914. Classes met four days a week from 3:00 to 5:00 p.m. and the men were encouraged to attend for one-hour periods. The course lasted a total of sixty-four hours and the curriculum concentrated mainly on reading, understanding and speaking English, and doing simple arithmetic.

Several factors hindered the progress of the class. The teacher was unable to speak Polish, the attitudes of the students were impassive and unresponsive, and the selection of material was poor. These factors would be recognized in the future as common barriers to effective literacy education.

It is not clear how extensively such programs were conducted. There are vague references to indicate that prior to 1920 factory classes were being conducted in Ohio, Michigan, Pennsylvania, Illinois, and Massachusetts as well as in New York and New Jersey. From lack of evidence in the records, one can probably surmise there was a general lack of interest in this problem on the part of industry, and classes were few in comparison to the number of business firms.

Mr. Somers, Chairman of the Board of Education in New York City, made this relevant comment: "I should be ashamed as an American citizen to read to you the list that I have in mind, of the industries, the firms,...the firms profiteering out of the opportunity that war gives, who absolutely refused us the chance to organize a class to teach the boys and girls in their employ who cannot speak the English language" (253: 28).

Federal concern about illiteracy

Draft reports with their shocking statistics made the federal government (and especially the Army) feel justifiably uneasy about the illiteracy problem. The government was now faced with two immediate national problems—an unpopular war and thousands of illiterate draftees. However, it was *not* the federal government, but Kentucky, that took initial action to remedy the situation. The Illiteracy Commission located all of those men who registered by making a mark and a special session of moonlight schools was started.

A statewide campaign to secure funds was initiated, teachers volunteered services, and special materials were prepared. The result was a text called *The Soldier's First Book*. The early lessons in the reader were simple explanations of why we were at war with Germany. A typical theme read (51: 90):

> Why are we at war?
> To keep our country free.
> To keep other people free.
> To make the world safe to live in.
> To stop the rule of kings.
> To put an end to war.

Shortly, under government auspices, a literacy campaign for illiterate registrants was initiated at Camp Taylor, Kentucky. Similar efforts followed in several other Army camps. In Spring 1918, the need for these schools was further emphasized. General Pershing, Commander of American Expeditionary Forces, issued an order to those at home to write letters to service persons to help boost low morale. The moonlight schools once again adjusted to the need, and illiterate relatives and friends were instructed along with the next group of men preparing for the draft (51: 101).

Professional Activities

Americanization presents a problem

Between 1915 and 1919, the Federal Bureau of Education provided the educational leadership for immigrant education programs. Under the direction of H. Wheaton and Fred Butler, extensive professional aid was given to organizations interested in this work.

In an effort to appraise the Americanization programs in terms of their relationship to the war, a conference was held on April 3, 1918. It was called by the Advisory Council on Americanization to the United States Bureau of Education. At the close of the conference, the Committee on Resolutions proposed the following suggestions (*253*: 36):

1. Cooperation was necessary at all levels of the government to carry out a complete Americanization program.
2. Industries were encouraged to cooperate in such efforts involving education.
3. Appropriations should be made by Congress to the proper agencies in order to implement such programs.
4. The schools in which elementary subjects were taught should be conducted in English only.

The suggestions made at the conference bore a striking similarity to the ideas proposed by the group in Passaic, New Jersey. But little was done about the problem because, in 1919, aid from the Bureau of Education stopped and immigrant education programs were on their own.

Methods and Materials

Materials for the foreign born illiterate

The abundance of instructional materials available for use with the foreign born makes it impossible to include them in this section. Since the main type of literacy education up to and including this period dealt with the foreign born, materials were not difficult to locate. *Teaching English to Aliens: A Bibliography of Textbooks, Dictionaries and Glossaries, and Aids to Librarians* (*268*) was published by the Bureau of Education. Based on the assumption that a common language tends to promote Americanism, the bibliography listed 1,078 books used especially with the foreign born.

Materials for the native born illiterate

Evidence indicates instructional materials for the native born illiterates were virtually nonexistent until the start of the moonlight schools. In her book, *Moonlight Schools for the Emancipation of Adults (51: 21)*, Stewart describes *The Rowan County School Messenger* and its function in instructing adults. The paper was unique in its concept. It enabled adults to read without humiliation and, at the same time, informed them about community activities. Unfortunately, there are no copies left for inspection save those stored away in attics.

The Country Life Readers (50) were prepared specifically to fill the void for instructional materials. The two books are written at a readability level of about 1.5 and 2.0 and deal with the problems of rural life. Each lesson is preceded by a list of new words and followed by a sentence to be copied by the students. Photographs and illustrations add interest.

The third significant book of this period, *The Soldier's First Book*, was described earlier. It also used a practical approach in presenting readings.

Professional publications

Three significant publications were produced by the Bureau of Education toward the close of this period. All were thorough, detailed, and had complete bibliographies. *Teaching English to the Foreign-Born* by Goldberger *(269)* describes in detail how to organize classes and how to use textbooks, and lists methods of teaching, professional suggestions for teachers, and sample lesson plans.

Community Americanization: A Handbook for Workers by Butler *(256)* includes specific instructions for organizing classes, philosophies involved in teaching the foreign born, and concrete suggestions for conducting a community literacy survey.

Butler's *State Americanization (267)* basically presents the role the state was expected to play in the assimilation of the immigrant and outlines, step by step, the manner in which it could be done.

Summary

The period from 1910 to 1919 was one of fluctuating interests and motivations. The spirit of reform brought with it the first efforts directed toward educating native born illiterates. Distrust of foreigners stimulated efforts toward Americanization, and the great numbers of illiterate soldiers motivated the concern of the federal government.

Motivated by the establishment of the moonlight schools in Kentucky, groups worked to established illiteracy commissions. The concept spread rapidly from state to state but, for most of the decade, was hampered by lack of funds.

Slowly, local legislation attempting to solve the problem began to appear. It varied in form from restricting the number of immigrants to providing teachers for illiterates. The attempts to provide legislation were often fought bitterly on both sides.

For the most part, the illiteracy problem was left to local talent. The federal government did display concern when the draft records revealed alarming numbers of illiterates at a national level, but it was basically the local governments that attacked the problem in its new form. With this new effort, the movement against illiteracy continued, assured that "adult illiteracy in the United States is doomed. A few years more and there will not be a vestige of it left" *(261: 12)*.

Chapter Three

1920-1929: Prosperity and Progress

Social Climate

Economic backdrop

The period following World War I was characterized by a desire to forget the problems of war and retreat from foreign affairs. The public was tired of conflict and goals stressed complacency, prosperity, and normalcy for the people and the country.

In October 1919, the stock market dropped and by 1920 the United States was experiencing economic distress. By 1921, 3.5 million persons were out of work. The plight of the farmers made the problem even more complicated. The economic recovery program undertaken by the administration included the reduction of taxes, governmental withdrawal from business, reduction in federal regulations, and aid to business and farmers. Whether it was the result of this program or just an eventual wearing out, the business depression was short-lived and was followed by good times.

The new age appears

As the recovery progressed, business revitalized and the visual symbols of a new age appeared. Business flourished, mass production made goods readily available, and spin-off businesses appeared. Signs of the new age were also visible in the educational system. In most states, schooling to age sixteen had been made compulsory by law. Small country schools were consolidated into larger systems and higher education, which had declined during the war years, was on the rise again.

Graduate schools began to appear at some of the universities. Because faculties were often responsible for research as well as teaching, several foundations (such as Carnegie and Rockefeller) sustained interest in schools, often in a financial manner.

The mood of America

The period of prosperity the country was experiencing was accompanied by an era of lawlessness, suspicion, and intolerance. The passing of the Eighteenth Amendment on Prohibition opened a vast new area of crime. The illicit liquor business, and its related activities, boomed during the decade as syndicates grew larger and more sophisticated in nature.

The success of the Bolshevik revolution in 1917 had shocked Americans and created a fear of Communism. People felt these radical ideas might be imported to this country by foreigners. These anxieties, and a basic desire to maintain a policy of isolation, prompted further action against immigration. Immigrant legislation was passed in 1921 and 1924. By 1930, the effects of this legislation were evident in the census; fewer immigrants were recorded.

An awareness of illiteracy

The statistics secured through the draft records, as well as the ever present difficulties in educating the immigrant population, brought the realization that something needed to be done about illiteracy. Although concern was expressed at a national level, little concrete action resulted from the alarm. Perhaps it was this national concern which motivated many states to move against illiteracy. It was during this period that state legislation was passed related to compulsory schooling, training of adult teachers, and, in some instances, funding the operation of illiteracy commissions.

One might also consider the times as a motivational factor for these local efforts. Recovery was rapid from the short depression at the turn of the decade; employment was high and people were relatively free from distressing responsibilities. With these prevailing conditions, there was time to deal with the more idealistic problems of the day.

The Statistics

The statistics on illiteracy revealed in the 1920 census bore little resemblance to the figures in the draft records. One reason for the difference probably had to do with how realistic a definition was used when discussing an illiterate. The Army needed men who could function with reading and writing, while the census was less demanding.

In 1920, the census defined an illiterate as any person age ten or over who was unable to write in any language, regardless of his ability to read (*230:* 1145). This definition automatically produced a large group of people classified as literate who, in actuality, were not able to read and write with a reasonable degree of facility. Thus, the dwindling percentages which appeared could be considered a surface phenomenon.

Neglectful census takers accounted in part for census errors. Often the assumption was made and recorded that because a person was white he was literate, or because he was foreign born or black, he was not. In many instances, the recorders were not at fault; some people were unwilling to admit to illiteracy and gave faulty information.

Whatever the drawbacks, the census information allows a comparison to be made with the previous decade. The figures, though not exact, provide a rough comparison of improvement or decline. In 1920, approximately 4,931,905 people were illiterate. This represented 6 percent of the population of the country and a decline of 1.7 percent from the previous census (*230:* 1150).

The subtotals of the census revealed drops in almost all classifications of illiterates. A decline from 30.4 percent to 22.9 percent was recorded for blacks. The percentage of all white illiterates dropped from 5 percent to 4 percent, while the native white illiterate population showed a drop from 3 to 2 percent (*230:* 1150).

An exception was the group of foreign born illiterates. Instead of a decrease, the census showed a slight increase in the number and percent of people in this group. In 1910, 12.7 percent or 1,650,361 foreign born illiterates were living in this country. By 1920, the figure had increased to 1,763,740 or 13.1 percent (*230:* 1150). The influx of immigrants during the prewar years was evident in the 1920 census.

The Bureau of the Census credited the drop in illiteracy rates to educational improvement. It noted that, when analyzing the information in terms of urban and rural illiteracy, the rural areas seemed to have experienced less improvement than the urban areas. Although there was no mention of the level at which the progress was made, an age analysis disclosed more literate persons in the younger age group. One can therefore suppose progress was primarily at the elementary and secondary levels and not at the adult education level.

Legislation

Although there was expressed national concern about illiteracy during this period, virtually no federal legislation was passed which related directly to the problem. For the most part, laws which were passed had only indirect bearings on national illiteracy. Those laws dealing more specifically with the problem were the results of the efforts of individual states.

The Cable Act

An example of related federal legislation was the Cable Act, passed on September 22, 1922 (*263:* 39). This legislation made it possible for alien women to be naturalized after marrying an American citizen or naturalized citizen.

The act produced a new need for women's Americanization and literacy classes. Since the obstacles of home duties and family were great, these classes needed to meet in social centers and neighborhood groups at hours conducive to the housewife's schedule. In many instances, child care facilities were needed to assure attendance.

The Emergency Immigration Act

The Emergency Immigration Act of 1921 and the United States immigration policy that followed probably affected illiteracy more than any other legislation passed during the decade. The act accomplished this by establishing a quota system. It "assigned to each nation an immigrant quota consisting of not more than 3 percent of the number of its nationals resident in the United States according to the census of 1910" (*28:* 684). Since the number of immigrants in the United States in 1910 was less than in 1920, the 1910 figures were selected as the working basis.

By 1924 the new immigration policy had emerged. Congress set the quota at 2 percent of the nationals in the United States in 1890. The result was a drastic reduction in the number of entering immigrants, especially from southern and eastern Europe. After July 1, 1927 the number of quota immigrants was limited to 150,000. Again, the toll was taken mainly in the less literate countries. Italy's quota was 5,802, while the Great Britain and Northern Ireland area quota was 65,721 (*28:* 685).

The Sterling-Reed Bill

The reader will note that the following section is a discussion of a bill and not a law which was passed. What makes this bill noteworthy of comment is its unique features related to literacy education. Introduced to Congress in 1924, it sought to create a Department of Education with one of the several functions of the department being to conduct research in the area of illiteracy.

The bill proposed not only moral support, but also financial support in this effort. Previously, financial aid for literacy programs had been provided through volunteer agencies, donations, and, occasionally, the state itself. Specifically the bill stated:

Section 7. In order to encourage the States to remove illiteracy $7,500,000, or so much thereof as may be necessary, is authorized to be appropriated annually for the instruction of illiterates fourteen years of age and older. Said sum shall be apportioned to the States which qualify under the provisions of the act, in the proportions which their respective illiterate population fourteen years of age and over, not including foreign-born illiterates, bear to such illiterate population of the United States, not including outlying possessions, according to the last preceding census of the United States. All funds apportioned to a State for the removal of illiteracy shall be distributed and administered in accordance with the laws of said State in like manner as the funds provided by State and local authorities of said State shall determine the course of study, plans, and methods for carrying out the purpose of this section within said State in accordance with the laws thereof (217: 3).

Section 8 of the bill provided for appropriations up to $7,500,000 for Americanization programs designed to teach immigrants to speak and read English. The states would be able to accept the provisions, provided the state or local authorities appropriated at least as much as the federal government (217: 6).

State law related to literacy education

By 1927, 60 percent of the states had enacted legislation encouraging adult education. Eleven states were cited for producing favorable results in this area. Their laws, which varied in form, are summarized below.

California's legislation required all illiterates between the ages of eighteen and twenty-one to attend school. In addition to this, the state maintained a literacy test for voters.

In Connecticut, school districts with more than 10,000 inhabitants were required by law to maintain evening schools for persons over age fourteen.

The Massachusetts State Department of Education worked in cooperation with towns seeking instruction for adults unable to speak, write, or read the language.

Minnesota allowed evening schools to be maintained as a part of the public school system. Any person sixteen years of age or older could attend if he was unable to attend day school.

In New York State, instruction was provided for the foreign

born, native illiterates, and minors over age sixteen. Classes were conducted during the day or evening and used a variety of facilities.

In Oregon, the education of the adult immigrant was supervised by the Department of Americanization. Programs originating from this source were a part of the public school system.

Pennsylvania's law stated that any school district was required to provide courses in adult education when it received written applications from twenty or more residents sixteen years of age or older. The requests had to be from residents not in attendance in day school.

In Rhode Island, public evening schools were required in every town with twenty or more students between ages sixteen and twenty-one who were unable to speak, read, or write English. Free continuation schools were provided for persons beyond compulsory attendance age. If a person between these ages was unable to meet the standards of English usage set up by the State Board of Education, he was then required to attend either day or evening school.

South Carolina employed a full-time state supervisor for the purpose of overseeing the schools established for illiterates.

The law in South Dakota required that persons unable to speak, read, or write English at a fifth grade level attend classes for this purpose.

The last of the eleven states, Tennessee, required local school districts to maintain evening schools for those individuals over age sixteen (*265:* 4-6).

It is probably worthwhile to note that these legal endeavors were disjointed efforts on the part of individual states. There was no central clearinghouse or organization to coordinate these efforts. In some states, legislation made education for illiterates compulsory; in others, education was optional or available only if requested by citizens. In five of the states, one-half the cost was met by the states.

Programs

A survey of programs

In May 1925, the general interest of the federal government in the problem of illiteracy expressed itself in a semiconcrete manner. The Commissioner of Education conducted a National Survey of State Programs of Adult Education. Forty-four out of forty-eight states responded. The results indicated that thirty-four states had enacted legislation dealing with adult education, though not necessarily literacy education. This legislation did not indicate the education was mandatory. It merely suggested there were state laws favoring adult education.

In many instances programs were funded locally, but in some cases the state provided financial aid to the local communities. In 1925, twenty-four states assumed this financial burden to some degree. In addition, twenty-seven states furnished leadership through state departments of education.

Recognizing the need for specially trained teachers for adults, fourteen states provided some type of teacher training courses. Active in this effort were California, Delaware, South Carolina, New York, Arkansas, Wisconsin, Massachusetts, Rhode Island, Connecticut, Oregon, North Dakota, Michigan, Maine, and Pennsylvania.

Finally, the survey revealed that in 1924, twenty-five states had approximately 286,000 students enrolled in classes for adult illiterates and the foreign born. It concluded that "despite waning interest in Americanization and the serious retrenchment policy in public expenditures, the school programs for native illiterates and adult foreign born have steadily improved during the past five years, and the general outlook for the Nation is most promising" (*251*: 5-6).

The opportunity schools of South Carolina

A discussion of local literacy programs for this period would be cumbersome and needlessly repetitive. The hundreds of individual efforts in communities throughout the country were all similar in nature. Teaching materials were available, but they were not specifically designed for adult literacy education. The teachers often taught elementary school children during the day and adults during the evening. Some programs were designed for the foreign born and for those interested in Americanization, while others were directed toward native born illiterates.

One local effort, which was to become better known in the thirties, was the "opportunity school" in South Carolina. Initiated in 1921 by the State Supervisor of Adult Education, the school had a unique feature. Its purpose was to provide instruction for illiterate girls and women. No men were admitted! The school was held in Tamasee, South Carolina, and had thirty-six students. The curriculum consisted of reading, writing, arithmetic, spelling, health, civics, good manners, and arts and crafts.

The favorable results of the program encouraged educators to open another school in 1922. This one, held at Lander College, provided instruction for eighty-nine students whose ages ranged from fourteen to fifty-one. The average previous schooling for these students was three years.

By 1923, an opportunity school at Erskine College was opened for men bringing the combined enrollment of the schools to 180 students. The schools continued to function and grow. In the early thirties, they were submitted to a critical study by the Carnegie Corporation of New York (23: 11-12).

Indian education

Although the records reveal very little about the educational progress made by the American Indians during this period, they do include a piece of significant legislation related to the problem. The Act of November 2, 1921 provided the needed authority to conduct an On-Reservation Indian Adult Education Program.

Basically this was a program of general education, including instruction in basic education through high school subjects. Because it was geared to help the Indian become active in community life, the program included such appropriate areas of study as driver education, budgeting, and home renting. The program was specifically aimed at those Indians who lacked a basic education (285: 63).

Professional Activities

During the twenties, those most concerned with illiteracy did much to direct the attention of the public and educators toward this problem. Their efforts recognized the reorganization of professional groups, expansion of state literacy campaigns, and a national meeting which shared ideas and common problems.

Illiteracy commissions

Illiteracy commissions were often established in conjunction with the campaigns. The primary purpose of a commission was to organize the campaign and solicit funds from individuals, organizations, and the government.

In 1921, Maine and North Dakota set out to "abolish illiteracy"; while, in 1922, Ohio established its illiteracy commission. Soon after, Virginia, West Virginia, Texas, Louisiana, Michigan, California, Minnesota, Oklahoma, and New Mexico became active in extending opportunities to their illiterates (51: 142-145).

National Education Association

During the period from 1915 to 1919, the Federal Bureau of Education was particularly active in providing the educational leadership in immigrant education programs. At the end of World War I the Bureau ceased providing this service because of inadequate funds. In 1920, the National Education Association organized a Department of Immigrant Education. The department expanded to include supervisors and teachers of native illiterates, and in 1924 changed its name to the National Department of Adult Education of the NEA (*241: 3*).

At the 1925 Indianapolis meeting, the NDAE supported the use of competitive exams for the position of Specialist in Adult Education in the United States Bureau of Education. The proponents believed such a person would strengthen the work nationally, coordinate efforts, and insure the development of adult education programs in states where illiterates had not had an opportunity to progress (*251: 11*).

National Illiteracy Conference

On January 11, 1924 an illiteracy conference was held in Washington, D.C. Representatives were present from each state, various organizations, and the government. The main purpose of the conference was to formulate programs for literacy work in the United States.

Charles M. Herlihy chaired a special committee which was asked to design a course of study and methods of instruction for illiterates. The resulting bulletin, *Elementary Instruction for Adults (259)*, was an extremely detailed endeavor in the areas of curriculum, teaching approaches, and materials for native illiterates. The concern for native born illiterates had found expression in the format of a practical and usable program.

The National Illiteracy Crusade

Although the records are not clear about its origin, the National Illiteracy Crusade conducted in 1924 appears to have received its impetus from the National Illiteracy Conference. The crusade was headed by John H. Finley of the *New York Times*.

Most likely the purpose of the crusade was to "eradicate illiteracy," but there is no evidence of its goal. The lack of materials concerning the crusade also makes it impossible to describe the approaches used in dealing with the problem and gives no indication of its failure or success. The vague references merely indicate there was a group of people, concerned about this problem at the national level, who made some attempt to organize and work with the problem (*86:* 877).

The Advisory Committee on National Illiteracy

In the waning days of 1929, President Hoover appointed an Advisory Committee on National Illiteracy with Secretary of Interior Ray Lyman Wilbur serving as chairperson. The primary function of the Advisory Committee was to ascertain facts and give advice to the National Advisory Committee on Education. The committee sought to discover what had been done in literacy education, to formulate literacy methods and techniques, and to determine what factors influenced illiteracy. In addition, it was interested in investigating the relationship of Americanization and illiteracy and the manner in which to deal with illiterate groups of Indians and Blacks (*57:* 807).

On December 17, 1929 the Advisory Committee made the illiteracy campaign a national one. The aim was to give five million adults an opportunity to learn to read and write before the 1930 census. The services of John H. Finley, head of the National Illiteracy Crusade, were enlisted (*86:* 877).

Descriptions concerning this campaign appear to be virtually nonexistent. One is able to say, however, that to provide five million adults with an opportunity to read and write in the course of two or three months was an unreasonable and idealistic goal. The financial support for such a monumental task amounted to $52,001.99. The total reflected the interest of individuals and small groups, since all the money resulted from correspondence and personal appeals. By its lack of appropriations, the federal government displayed its academic interest in the problem (*162:* 244).

Professional evaluation

The definition of illiteracy was relatively consistent until the twenties. Basically, a person who could read and write was literate; one who could not, was illiterate. During the twenties, educators began to question this type of definition. Was it really an adequate way to evaluate literacy? "No," was the answer arrived at by some people.

In 1924, at a National Council for Education meeting, one educator defined an illiterate in this manner: "Clearly from a practical social point of view it is one who has not mastered the art of reading and writing sufficiently to use it in daily life" (*151:* 248). He went on to emphasize that no data had ever been collected based on that type of definition.

At the annual National Education Association meeting in 1929 the question of definition arose again. In one presentation a speaker proclaimed:

As educators we violently object to classifying as literate, as we do now, those who can write their names only. There is a real chance that column seventeen of the 1930 census will be changed by the government to read "whether able to read English understandingly" with instructions to the enumerators to inquire as to the ability to read the American newspapers—the equivalent of fourth grade English (*108*: 285).

The changes suggested by the speaker did not come about by the 1930 census, but the embryo of an idea had formed and during the next two decades developed into something more specific and demanding.

Methods and Materials

Professional publications

At the turn of the decade, the Carnegie Corporation conducted a study which concluded that special training was needed for teaching adults and that teacher training courses ought to be developed. In 1920, the United States Bureau of Education published a course of study to be used in training such teachers. *Training Teachers for Americanization (270)* included discussions on recruiting students, organizing factory classes, use of community agencies, techniques for teaching, and outlines for subject areas. An extensive bibliography of professional and instructional books was included.

In 1925 it produced *Elementary Instruction for Adults (259)*, a course of study for illiterate adults (described earlier in this book).

In 1927 the Bureau prepared a manual to be used in extension courses for teachers. The title of this work was *Methods of Teaching Adult Aliens and Native Illiterates for Use in Colleges, Universities and Normal Schools, and for Teachers of Adults (263)*. The text was divided into five major sections: Americanization, organization, methods of teaching, special classes, and background needs for a literacy teacher. Each section was suitable for a full course of instruction.

The Bureau updated the course of study in 1928 and produced a revision entitled *Helps for Teachers of Adult Immigrants and Native Illiterates (260)*. The format was very similar to its predecessor and both books included extended bibliographies.

Instructional materials

Although the Bureau of Education provided literacy teachers with several bibliographic sources to aid teaching, instructional materials were still difficult to locate. The need for simple readable books was fundamental. In 1929, the American Library Association researched the problem and published *Readable Books in Many Subjects* (*3: 76*). This list included 369 books which could be used for adult instruction but were not specifically designed for adult use. In the few instances when they were, the instructional level was not often lower than grade three.

For this reason, the *Bible Story Reader* (*31*) was a unique contribution in the area of instructional materials. Published in 1922, it was first used in North Carolina. The reader featured stories from the Old and New Testaments and ranged in difficulty from level one to level five.

Instructional methods

The instructional methods used during the twenties indicated some changes in pedagogical thinking. The choral recitation approach was probably still used extensively, but more emphasis was being placed on recitation with "understanding."

The publications from the Bureau of Education stressed the need for teaching approaches that would not offend adults. They also emphasized the adult's need for a method which yielded a useful skill almost immediately.

Although these were the ideals, it was quite a while before methods and materials became sophisticated enough to accomplish this task.

Summary

For the major portion of the twenties the people of the United States experienced economic good times. Employment was high, credit easy to obtain, and modern conveniences produced leisure time.

Fear about Communism and the experiences during World War I resulted in a desire on the part of the people to be isolated. These experiences revealed themselves more concretely in the anti-foreign born attitudes and the fear that foreign ideas were radical ideas. Perhaps all these conditions explain, to some degree, why this was such a rapidly moving and changing period.

The federal government's concern for the illiterate was displayed in its numerous publications which offered professional advice to those interested in the problem. Activity at a state level was even more intense and implemented with state aid and special teachers.

Professional groups and organizations were particularly active in making contributions to literacy education. Literacy campaigns were stimulated by committees, the National Education Association reorganized in order to accommodate supervisors and teachers of native illiterates, and a National Illiteracy Conference was conducted. The conference may well have been the stimulus for a National Illiteracy Crusade organized in 1924.

At the close of the decade, President Hoover appointed an Advisory Committee on National Illiteracy. Its purpose was to collect facts and make suggestions for the Committee on Education. This was the first national committee to be formed for such a purpose.

The period, then, was one of yet uncoordinated projects and efforts with some attempt to share ideas and knowledge. The economic conditions made it possible for people to have time for and interest in the more hidden problems of the day. But a depression followed soon and the enthusiasm of crusaders, educators, and a concerned public was directed toward more immediate problems than illiteracy.

Chapter Four

1930-1939: New Deal America

Social Climate

The great depression

During the 1928 presidential campaign Hoover had promised to triumph over poverty. But the long period of speculation, agricultural and industrial overexpansion, and easy credit was near an end. By the time Hoover entered office in 1929, a depression was probably inevitable. Great declines in auto sales and building and the increased efficiency in machines were beginning to take their toll in terms of the unemployed. In addition, margin buying in the stock market and the lack of balance in international trade helped set the stage for economic failure. The crash finally came in October 1929 and with it prices dropped, factories shut down, and banks closed. By 1930 approximately seven million people were unemployed.

The New Deal

As the economic structure crumbled, the people of the country rapidly lost confidence in Hoover's administration. The 1932 campaign foreshadowed his defeat. Roosevelt attacked Hoover for his spending and, at the same time, proposed relief for the unemployed with public works programs. When the returns were in, Hoover met with an overwhelming defeat.

Roosevelt's administration was characterized by controversial legislation. These reform laws affected the farmer, industry, planned economy, banks, and the individual at a most personal level.

Several laws were designed to provide work and a minimal income for thousands of unemployed. In 1933 the Federal Emergency Relief

Administration provided money for either work relief or direct relief payments. The Civil Works Administration provided the work relief jobs. In 1935, the Works Progress Administration assumed this task. Between 1935 and 1941, over eight million workers were employed in WPA projects.

The National Youth Administration supplemented the work of the WPA. For those in school, it provided noninstructional work for small wages; and for youth not in school, it provided part-time jobs.

In still another attempt to provide employment, the Civilian Conservation Corps was initiated in 1933. The conservation camps were designed to provide work for unmarried men between the ages of eighteen and twenty-five.

Roosevelt's programs had greatly extended the power of the Executive Branch, caused heated controversies, and created a national debt twice the size of that in Hoover's administration. The President and his policies were either held in high esteem or strongly disliked, and his popularity vacillated as the country struggled through the depression years. One could safely say that "save Washington's first administration and the Civil War years, no other comparable period had witnessed such changes in American life" (28: 761).

The Statistics

The 1930 census

The 1929 proposal of the National Education Association to establish a fourth grade education as a basis for literacy was not adopted in the 1930 census. The criteria for literacy remained vague and liberal as the Bureau of the Census returned to the definition used in 1900. In 1900 and 1930 the bureau defined an illiterate as "any person ten years of age or over who is not able to read and write, either in English or in some other language" (229: 1219). According to this definition, 4.3 percent of the persons in this country over ten years of age were illiterate. This percentage represented 4,283,753 individuals (229: 1223). When compared to the previous census data, a 1.7 percent decline was evident. In actual numbers, there were 648,152 fewer illiterates in 1930 than in 1920.

The illiteracy figures for the white population dropped from 4.0 percent to 2.7 percent. For the blacks, the decline was even greater. In 1920, 22.9 percent were illiterate while in 1930 only 16.3 percent were classified in this manner. The difference in rates of the two races was demonstrated in still another manner. In the North and West, where the black population was not great, the illiteracy rate was 2.7 percent. The South, which had a larger concentration of blacks, reported that 8 percent of the population was unable to read and write (*91*: 641).

The attempts during the twenties to restrict immigration were beginning to demonstrate their effectiveness by the 1930 census. Legislation curtailed some of the immigrant traffic, but the most effective measure was the quota system. With this technique in effect, the majority of newcomers were from northern and western Europe, the areas containing the more literate countries (*222*: 116-117).

The actual figures provided proof of the success of the system. In 1920, 13.1 percent of the foreign born people living in the United States were illiterate. This percentage represented 1,763,740 individuals (*230*: 1150). By 1930, the number of foreign born illiterates dropped to 1,304,084 or 9.9 percent of the foreign born population in the United States (*229*: 1223).

Another view

The census records from 1900 through 1930 indicate a steady decline in the numbers and percentages of illiterates in the United States. Since all four censuses used a similar definition for illiteracy, and since 1930 is the last time such a definition is used, this decade provides a likely place to pause and view illiteracy progress in another way.

To the casual glance, there is a very impressive rate of progress. In 1900, 10.7 percent of the population was illiterate. Using the same definition in 1930, only 4.3 percent of the people were unable to read and write. A drop of 6.4 percent occurred during the thirty-year period. One could say that illiteracy had been cut by more than 50 percent.

But it is important to note that the number of illiterates did not decrease by 50 percent. In 1900 there were 6,180,069 illiterates while in 1930 the number was 4,283,753. Even with these figures it is difficult to envision the actual gains made in literacy education. However, if the difference of these two figures is divided by the thirty years they span, the resulting figure will indicate the illiteracy loss on a yearly basis. The results are surprising. Each year the illiteracy figure was lowered by only 63,210 individuals—enough people to fill a medium-sized football stadium.

Legislation

Legislation during the thirties centered around relief, recovery, and, in some instances, reform. The efforts directed toward illiteracy evidenced in the twenties were not present during the thirties. Although no legislation dealt specifically with the problem, there were several programs relating to illiteracy which were the results of the "relief legislation." These are described in the section on literacy programs.

Programs

The opportunity schools of South Carolina

The opportunity schools of South Carolina had been in operation for ten years when, in 1931, the Carnegie Corporation of New York granted $5,000 for a study to evaluate the program. The specific purpose of the study was to determine what progress could be made by adults with limited education when favorable conditions for learning were provided.

The summer session was under the direction of William S. Gray. One session for white persons was held at Clemson College in Calhoun, South Carolina; the other session for blacks was held at Seneca Junior College in Seneca, South Carolina. The enrollment at Clemson was 233 and in Seneca it was 55.

A four week program was conducted with reading, writing, spelling, math, history, civics, and personal grooming forming the core of the curriculum. Organized physical education classes, tours, and musical groups rounded out the program.

The study concluded that 1) the greatest handicap of the program was the lack of simple, well-graded materials and that materials related to contemporary problems were probably most useful; and 2) the informal training in the program was as important as the formal training, with the possibility that this informal training increased the rate at which gains could be made. Finally, the report suggested that the instructional methods used were too closely patterned for children and that adults needed different procedures in order to achieve success (23).

Other state programs

States continued the literacy programs originated in the twenties. However, new programs dealing with work relief also left an impact on literacy education.

In 1933 every major city in California maintained classes for illiterates. These classes were organized in conjunction with a State Department of Education plan. Once the program was set up by the department, materials were developed and a program of teacher training was established. A state committee was then organized and it included representatives from organizations interested in illiteracy. Finally, a program of supervision was conducted to aid in evaluation. In an attempt to insure the success of the program, the incoming population was surveyed for illiterates (*131*: 559).

In Alabama, teacher training institutes were held for white and black teachers who expected to instruct adults. Under the auspices of the Alabama State Department of Education some counties offered as many as 120 hours of instruction for illiterate prisoners.

An intensive program in elementary education for adults originated in Washington, D.C. Although the program was open to native born illiterates, the enrollment was mostly foreign born. The program provided day and night classes, transportation, child care, and home instruction (*272*: 431).

Work Relief in Education

In 1932 a variation of a public works program was created in New York City. It was called Work Relief in Education and was under the supervision of Harry L. Hopkins. The basic idea of the program was to utilize the unemployed to teach the unemployed.

In December 1932, free classes were initiated for the unemployed of New York City. Approximately 10,000 students and 250 instructors were involved in the experiment. Although the program was not designed for illiterates, there were provisions for those who desired courses in elementary education. The Relief Administration appropriated a sum of $30,000 for salaries to carry on the work while individuals and institutions provided housing and equipment for the experimental venture (*60*: 717).

Federal Emergency Relief Administration

The Federal Emergency Relief Administration was created in 1933. Because of his Work Relief in Education project in New York, Roosevelt appointed Harry Hopkins as the administrator of the FERA. Hopkins held that work relief was psychologically better for an individual, and the best way to gain respect and to work off relief was through education. With the cooperation of the United States Commissioner of Education, George F. Zook, a national program of work relief was launched.

The Civil Works Administration which came into existence as a branch of the Federal Emergency Relief Administration, functioned as the agency which created and aided the work projects. The nature of these projects was varied and some were directly related to education.

For example, work relief for teachers in rural areas was provided in places where schools had closed or would be closed without funds. In some instances, money was available so that men and women could be taught to read and write English. With this project, special emphasis was placed on teaching those under the age of fifty-five. In addition, funds were appropriated for general adult education. In this instance, the program also supplied funds for other related areas such as vocational education, instructing the disabled, and establishing nursery schools in areas where there were great numbers of unemployed (60: 718).

The programs sponsored by the Federal Emergency Relief Administration were present in many communities in the country, and probably met with varying degrees of success. One survey of literacy classes established by the FERA was conducted in Georgia. The sample consisted of seven counties, or 77,605 people. About 1,891 illiterates (33.8 percent of the total illiterate population) were attending classes. The survey further disclosed that only 13.2 percent of the illiterates on relief were attending classes (169: 515).

The survey concluded that

> the FERA classes for illiterates are apparently reaching only a small part of the population for whom they are intended. This seems particularly true when one thinks of the illiterates on relief. Lack of attendance at literacy classes seems largely the result of inaccessibility of classes, although in some cases indifference to opportunity seems to be involved. Although the literacy classes are not doing the job as well as they might, they are doing a job which was not done at all before they were organized (169: 517).

The Georgia survey revealed attitude as a major problem in literacy education. Although it was probably one of the first times this factor was mentioned, future programs would arrive at similar conclusions. Time and time again, a general indifference on the part of the undereducated would be displayed.

Works Progress Administration

The task of providing work relief was handed over to the Works Progress Administration in 1935. Harry Hopkins headed the administration and L.R. Alderman was the National Director of Education for the WPA.

One large educational project of the WPA dealt specifically with illiteracy. In the summer of 1936, Dr. Alderman announced plans for an illiteracy campaign in New York City. The project involved the WPA, social agencies, and the New York City Board of Education. The campaign was conducted for a period of four years with approximately 3,000 teachers involved in the work (87: 686).

In 1938, the Works Progress Administration announced that more than one million illiterate persons had been taught to read and write and plans were made to enlarge the program. In addition, WPA teachers planned to prepare a series of readers for adults that would differ radically from materials used previously. "The new readers will take subjects of normal adult interest, such as health, safety, occupation, family life and government, and present them in simple, assimilable form" (55: 693).

The programs of the Works Progress Administration continued and by 1941 had provided employment for over eight million people, approximately one-fifth of the country's workers. Finally, in 1941, the WPA was terminated by the war.

The Civilian Conservation Corps

Another relief project, initiated in March 1933, was the Civilian Conservation Corps. The main purpose of this organization was to provide work for unmarried men between the ages of eighteen and twenty-five. The volunteers could enroll for a period of one year.

The work program was originally designed to conserve the natural resources of the country, but grew to the point where some form of education and training was desirable for the young men. The educational program established was vocational in nature with courses in auto mechanics, electricity, plumbing, and wood working. The skills provided by these courses were useful in "camp life" as well as in life outside the corps.

Along more academic lines, a study of the reading ability of CCC enrollees revealed that their ability to read lagged behind age and formal training. While the men ranged in ages from eighteen to twenty-five, their average reading age was only 11.8 years. This represented an average reading level of grade 6.8 (177: 101).

Still more surprising facts were exposed when a second survey revealed that 1.9 percent of the enrollees in CCC camps were illiterate. Of the 375,000 men tested, 7,369 were unable to read a newspaper or write a letter.

Armed with this information, a program in basic education was developed for the undereducated enrollee. As one might expect, the emphasis was placed on early reading, writing, and arithmetic. No phase of the educational program was compulsory, but the illiterate men were approached and urged to attend class.

Instructional materials were designed for the educational program as well as manuals for instructors. The manuals included information on learning and teaching, and ideas for effective teaching and lesson planning. The guides for the vocational subjects were quite detailed. They included lesson plans complete with questions, procedures, assignments, and references (*275*).

Although the major emphasis in the program was vocational, some progress was made in literacy education. During the single year from June 1934 to June 1935, the Civilian Conservation Corps reported that 4,339 men had learned to read (*166*: 868).

Professional Activities

Advisory Committee on National Illiteracy

The Advisory Committee on National Illiteracy, appointed by President Hoover in 1929, operated on meager contributions into the early thirties. But by January 1933 the funds were exhausted and the committee concluded its work. In the course of its investigations, the committee completed seven studies, each dealing with a different phase of the illiteracy problem:

1. A study of techniques for teaching illiterates.
2. A state by state survey of appropriations used for the education of illiterates.
3. An analysis of state and local laws related to illiterate drivers and accidents.
4. A study of the expected life span of the illiterate and his years of potential service if educated.
5. A study of white illiterates in the mountains of Virginia.
6. A survey of Indian attitudes regarding attempts to teach them.
7. A study of the relationship between illiteracy and crime.

In addition to these studies, the committee sent representatives to forty-four states for the purpose of consulting with State Education Departments and with prison authorities. As a direct result of these visits, a campaign was launched in 1932 to teach illiterate prisoners in South Carolina. Until that time, no educational work of any sort had been done in that state's prisons. In a similar spirit, North Carolina appointed a Director of Education for its prisons.

As its work terminated, the committee reported they felt the people of the United States were more "literacy conscious." The committee noted that results of campaigns were noticeable at the county level. In 1920 there were 100 counties in the country with 25 percent or more of their population illiterate. By 1930 only 26 such counties existed (*162*: 244).

This observation emphasized the fact that most of the literacy progress was still being achieved at a local level and that it was this local action which eventually made the difference in an illiteracy statistic. The work of the committee represented an attempt to discover the causes for illiteracy and to appraise the severity of the problems resulting from illiteracy. It also represented the first sustained and coordinated attempt to assess the problem.

Professional evaluation

As early as 1924 and 1929 concern was expressed about the criteria used in defining an illiterate, and the problem arose again in the thirties. Educators felt "ability to read and write" was a definition too open to personal interpretation.

At its annual convention in 1930, the National Education Association decided that a program for literacy should aim at the sixth grade level as a basis for literacy. This was a radical suggestion which was not immediately accepted by all organizations and agencies, but which did predict future trends (*129*: 490).

In 1933 William S. Gray attacked the illiteracy problem in an address to the National Education Association. In the course of his speech he noted reasons to be dissatisfied with the results of the 1930 census reports on literacy. The first was that the definition used was extremely liberal. Second, inaccurate reports were often given to the census taker. He went on to say that, regardless of the census figures, 20 percent of the population in the United States was unable to read a newspaper. He emphasized the need to maintain a literacy level once it had been achieved, and described the failure of the semiliterate to read and increase his personal efficiency.

Gray proposed that any attack on illiteracy needed to deal with three levels of illiterates: 1) those who had not attained technical literacy, 2) those who were not functionally literate, and 3) those who were functionally literate but needed to enrich their background (*122*: 280).

In order to achieve this end, he felt professional educational procedures were needed. The pioneer method of campaigns still had its place in planning a program but, in itself, was not an adequate way to meet the illiteracy problem.

A final thought on the subject emphasized a point made as far back as the moonlight schools of Kentucky: "In teaching those who are illiterate, major emphasis should be given to those types of instruction that will provide a broader understanding of practical everyday problems, that will increase their personal and social efficiency, and that will stimulate new interests and aspirations" (*122*: 281).

Professional research and inquiries

It was during the thirties that early attempts at research in literacy education began to take place. Although these efforts were far from sophisticated, they supported the thesis that professional educators were beginning to recognize their responsibility in the area of literacy education, and that volunteer campaigns could not always provide what was needed. Instead of doing "just anything" for the undereducated people, educators began to be concerned about the "best way" to do something, and about what obstacles needed to be overcome.

Investigations were sporadic and varied in nature as evidenced below. As noted earlier in this chapter, a study was conducted at the opportunity schools in South Carolina. The purpose of the investigation was to determine what progress could be made by undereducated adults. A survey of Federal Emergency Relief Administration literacy classes conducted in Georgia revealed that those who would benefit most by such classes did not participate. The Civilian Conservation Corps also conducted surveys which discovered large numbers of enrollees functioning below anticipated levels and an extensive number of illiterates. The Advisory Committee on National Literacy conducted seven studies during the period from 1930 to 1933. The topics under investigation ranged from causes of illiteracy to the relationship between crime and illiteracy.

In the course of its work, the Advisory Committee on National Illiteracy had the opportunity to consult with officials at prisons in forty-five states. This may be the reason that the problem of illiteracy in penal institutions received some attention during this period, and rightfully so. The problem of inmate illiteracy was a very extensive one. Institutions where there were large numbers of blacks had high illiteracy rates, and prisons in the South generally showed a higher degree of illiteracy than those in the North. A study of 2,500 inmates in a Virginia Penitentiary, State Farm, and Road Camps revealed 877 or 35 percent had no schooling. An additional 35 percent had failed to reach the fifth grade (39: 58-59).

Austin MacCormick, who disclosed some special problems in a study sponsored by the American Association for Adult Education, stated:

> The major fault of academic schools in our penal institutions is that when they attempt more than work for beginners only they lose sight of the principles of individualization and adhere too closely to the curriculum of the public grade school, either because of a state law requiring that all prisoners shall be given a fifth or eighth grade

education or because it is easier to copy an existing curriculum than to devise one really adapted to their needs. The result of the effort to give a fifth grade education is usually that the prisoners get a fifth rate education (39: 50).

The study also showed that time was a major problem in educating prisoners. Approximately 150,000 men were long term prisoners, but there were more than three times as many short termers. Since the early weeks of instruction usually progressed slowly, often there was not enough time to develop basic skills. Time was also a factor in the daily schedule. With an established prison routine, there was not enough time for study (147: 277).

MacCormick also discovered that inadequate methods, materials, and physical facilities hindered the progress of the student. As a solution to the problem he suggested that leadership was the key to a successful educational program. Prison directors should call on state and national organizations for aid. The State Department of Education could survey conditions and set up programs. Finally, educators needed to seek out the best materials available to help insure success.

Methods and Materials

Instructional materials

Once again, in the thirties, the need for adequate and appropriate instructional materials was stressed by educators, but the pleas seemed to fall on deaf ears of publishers. Low readability materials, keyed to the interests and needs of adults, were available only if those involved with programs produced them. *Day by Day at Clemson (23: 49)* was one such book. The content of the book was related to life at the opportunity schools and also contained such selections as community life, health, and family living. The book was mimeographed and, unfortunately, copies are no longer available for inspection.

It appears that a set of readers produced by teachers of the Works Progress Administration may have suffered a similar fate. They, too, were written in a simple, assimilable form and dealt with such useful topics as safety, occupations, and family life (55: 693).

The Civilian Conservation Corps designed a set of readers for literacy education when it expanded its program. *The* CCC *Camp Life Readers and Workbook (274)* provided some of the enrollees with their first introduction to the printed word. The basic theme of the books dealt with camp life and adjustment to it. An elementary reading program was designed to be completed in six books.

The format of each book was similar. Each lesson contained a story, word drill, and writing exercise. In later books, language usage was included. The books were designed to be used twice a week for three months. Type in the initial book was large, while the remaining five books were printed in standard type. Black and white illustrations were included for interest.

The drawback to the series was the fact that the vocabulary load was fairly large, provided for little repetition, and progressed at a fairly rapid rate. In spite of these shortcomings, the readers were one of the few materials which fulfilled the necessary qualifications cited by authorities.

The real value of this practical type of material became evident in the late fifties and sixties when publishers started producing materials with similar formats.

Summary

When Franklin D. Roosevelt entered office in 1933, the country was experiencing the full shock of the depression. During his administration, Roosevelt greatly extended the powers of the Executive Branch of the government and initiated controversial programs—all of which aroused intense feelings in the public.

States continued to develop illiteracy commissions but at a much slower pace than during the twenties. In some instances, the state even appropriated funds for this purpose. Federal programs involving illiterates were designed primarily to provide work relief. In the course of their operation, however, educational opportunities were provided for illiterates. The Work Relief in Education Project in New York City was an example of this type of program. Literacy classes were conducted through the Federal Emergency Relief Administration in hundreds of communities throughout the United States. Finally, the Civilian Conservation Corps—originally designed to provide work for young men—extended its educational program to include basic elementary education instruction for those who wished to participate.

The professional educator became more aware of his responsibilities during the thirties as evidenced in the following manner. First of all, criteria used to define an illiterate were questioned and suggestions were made for more stringent criteria. The success of these pressures would be evidenced in the forties.

Second, the basic problems involved in teaching illiterate adults were not yet solved. Initial efforts at research attempted to evaluate and answer some of these questions. The Advisory Committee on National Literacy also completed several investigations related to the illiteracy problem. Finally, many educators became active in producing the instructional materials needed by their students.

By the end of the period, it was fairly evident that campaigns conducted by volunteers were not adequate in solving the illiteracy problem; professional help was needed. The transition from volunteers to professional educators would not be immediate. With the war in Europe and the participation of the United States in it, one could almost foresee what would happen. The tremendous drain on manpower and the rapid training of draftees and volunteers would reveal that the problem of illiteracy had been discussed, but not conquered. The next few years would find much of the literacy training shifting from civilians to the military.

Chapter Five

1940-1949: The World in Crises

Social Climate

World tension and war

In the years prior to December 1941 the United States, still concerned with its domestic problems, tried to avoid foreign entanglement. The European countries were at war, and some Americans were willing to take a chance with a Hitler victory rather than to actively enter the conflict. Others, including President Roosevelt, advocated aid in many forms as long as it fell short of war.

But the world situation became so foreboding that a National Defense Advisory Commission was set up to ready the nation in case of war and, in September 1940, a Selective Service Act was adopted. The United States also leased eight bases from the British government in exchange for American destroyers. Although the United States reaffirmed its antiwar policy, it appeared ready for war.

Although many war defense measures were taken by the United States, Americans were totally unprepared for the disastrous attack on Pearl Harbor, December 7, 1941. Within twenty-four hours, Congress declared war on Japan. Shortly afterwards, Germany and Italy declared war on the United States. When America made similar declarations against the Axis Powers, the United States was at last deeply and morally committed to the war (*28:* 790-795).

Illiteracy and the war

The United States soon found itself in the middle of a wartime economy and domestic problems faded into the background as all energy was concentrated on the war effort. Illiteracy, however, was not shelved until a later date. In fact, it was not long after Pearl Harbor that the federal government became active in dealing with the problem, but it was at a military level and not a civilian one.

Even before the United States actually entered the war, a spotlight was thrown on the problem and the extent of its seriousness. The most immediate factor noted was the absence of a literacy requirement to enter the service. Approximately 347,000 persons were unable to write their names in the two registrations prior to Pearl Harbor, and 60,000 illiterates entered the service a half year prior to the war. The few feeble attempts to teach them proved fruitless (62: 598).

On May 14, 1941 a directive stated that induction would be refused to any individual unable to pass an examination of approximately fourth grade difficulty (116: 77). The results were shocking. In only six weeks, 55,000 persons were deferred because they were functionally illiterate. By September 1941 over 140,000 had been refused induction. The United States was faced with the same problem it had faced during World War I.

The May regulation accounted for rejection of 38 out of every 1,000 white inductees and 112 out of every 1,000 black inductees (62: 599). The situation soon stimulated the Southern states to exert political pressure since the refusals led to taking most of the white males between the ages of twenty and forty-four (175: 77).

This situation was accentuated when Pearl Harbor was bombed in December 1941. The strain for manpower was being felt on the fronts and in the war industries. On May 29, 1942, President Roosevelt reported that 433,000 men who would have been placed in class 1-A, eligible for immediate service, had been deferred "because of inability to meet the Army's literacy requirement" (64: 633). This number constituted enough men to compose fifteen army divisions.

By August 1942, the need for manpower had become so great that a new directive was passed. The Army announced that if a registrant was able to understand English and had enough intelligence to absorb military training, he would be eligible for induction. In order to prevent large concentrations of illiterates, only 10 percent of the white and 10 percent of the black registrants applying for enlistment in one day could be placed in this category. By October 14, 1942, approximately 135,000 illiterates had been taken into the service (62: 599).

The problem of illiteracy in the military became an even greater problem. The United States Navy had always been composed of volunteers and, as a result, was able to maintain high educational standards. But on December 5, 1942, a Presidential order stopped voluntary enlistments and gave the Selective Service the responsibility for supplying individuals for the Navy. In addition, the Navy had decided to accept black persons into the service. Thousands of individuals who were unable to meet literacy requirements were now being placed in the Navy as well as in the Army.

On February 1, 1943, after reappraising the illiteracy problem, the military announced that "the Army would now accept educationally deficient selectees not to exceed 5 percent of the total number of men accepted and assigned to the Army by color at each induction center on each day" (62: 600). By June 1943, the rejection rate had become so high that it was evident something had to be done about the manpower problem. Therefore, all persons who passed the intelligence exam, whether literate or not, were accepted in the service.

The postwar period

The people, unwilling to change leaders in the midst of a crisis, reelected Roosevelt for a fourth term in 1944. However, when Roosevelt died in April 1945, it was Harry S Truman who guided the United States into the postwar period. Returning to a peacetime economy was no simple task. Thousands of GIs flooded the job market. Large cancellations of government contracts created unemployment, and industrial strikes threatened to paralyze the economy. When the strikes brought about higher wages and price controls were removed, the result was inflation and, once again, the United States found itself struggling with its domestic problems.

In the postwar years, the United States established its role as a future leader in international affairs. The Marshall Plan, the conferences at Potsdam and Yalta, and the Berlin airlift were indicative of this emerging leadership (28: 835-845).

The Statistics

The 1940 census

In order to appraise the illiteracy situation in the United States in 1940, one should bear in mind that there were no actual figures for that census. Prior to the 1940 census, data were collected on the literacy of persons based on ability to read and write. At that time it was considered a suitable manner in which to appraise the educational level of the United States population. In 1940, in an attempt to obtain a more comprehensive view, the literacy question was replaced by data on the highest grade of school completed.

Since no illiteracy statistics existed for 1940, the figures used for comparison in this section are estimates of "what the 1940 illiteracy rate would have been if the 1947 illiteracy-education relationship had prevailed in 1940 also" (233: 3). According to those calculations, 3,249,000 individuals ten years of age and older (or 2.9 percent of this population) were unable to read and write in any language (233: 4). This indicated that there were approximately one million fewer illiterates in 1940 than in 1930.

The estimated figures for illiteracy resembled closely some of the figures available from the 1940 census. If one calculated the number of individuals age ten and over who had no schooling in 1940, the resulting figure would be approximately 3,100,000. This number corresponded closely to the estimated number unable to read and write (237: 42-78).

Using the same definition, the report showed that approximately 2.0 percent of the white population was illiterate, while 11.5 percent of the nonwhite population was classified in this manner. The decline in the number of foreign born illiterates continued with an estimated 9.0 percent present in the United States in 1940 (233: 4).

Future censuses included illiteracy information based on age fourteen. For that reason, it is probably helpful to note that the 1947 survey also estimated the number of illiterates fourteen years and older for the year 1940. According to the approximation, 4.2 percent of the people in the United States were unable to read and write. This represented 4,218,000 individuals (233: 4). Approximately three million individuals age fourteen or older had no schooling. This was about 3.0 percent of the population. About 11.5 million, or 11.6 percent, had either no schooling or less than five years (239: I-421).

Another appraisal of illiteracy

In October 1947 the United States Bureau of the Census collected specific information on illiteracy. It was in this survey that

> the question on illiteracy was asked for the first time in connection with the highest grade of school completed. It was assumed, however, that practically all of the illiterates would be among those who had completed less than five years of school and that all persons completing five years of school or more were literate (233: 2).

Although it was impossible to define illiteracy for an individual in terms of grade completion, it was possible to use it as a general indicator for large populations. This was probably how the term "functional illiteracy" came to be used in the 1947 survey. A functional illiterate was one who had completed fewer than five years of elementary school. The definition implied there was a lack of ability to comprehend simple instructions.

The 1947 survey revealed that the change from the conventional literacy definition to a more rigorous one presented an entirely different view of the illiteracy problem in the United States. In 1947, 8.2 million persons fourteen years of age and older had completed less than fifth grade; thus, they were classified as functionally illiterate. There were only 2.8 million in the survey who were unable to read and write.

The figures gave only an approximation of the actual situation. For example, among those persons with no schooling, 20 percent were literate according to a census type definition. At the other extreme, among those who had completed four years of school, about 5 percent were counted as illiterate. The report concluded that "the mere ability to read and write—perhaps with difficulty—is in itself an index of only limited usefulness" (233: 3).

The severity of the illiteracy problem may be visualized in still another manner. The 1940 census reported there were about ten million functionally illiterate adults aged twenty-five and over. This accounted for 13.5 percent of this adult population. The startling fact is that this figure represented *more* than the combined adult population of California, Oregon, Washington, Idaho, Montana, Nevada, Utah, Arizona, New Mexico, Wyoming, Colorado, North Dakota, South Dakota, and Nebraska. If all the ten million illiterates were concentrated in only these fourteen states, illiteracy would be recognized as a national problem and millions of dollars would be spent to remedy the situation. Since this population was scattered, few serious efforts were directed toward a solution (155: 92).

Programs and Materials

The United States had been shocked once before by the great number of individuals who were illiterate as they entered the service. But once World War I ended, the concern of the military subsided and the problem was virtually forgotten. The tremendous drain on manpower created by World War II brought about a new awareness of this problem. Because of the mobile nature of the war, servicemen had to be able to read diagrams, order and assemble machinery, and read maps. Even the war industries needed literate personnel, since they were so highly mechanized and technical. Arthur J. Altmeyer, Chairman of the Social Security Board, emphasized this fact. He stated: "The cost of machine breakdown and national spoilage is far too great in terms of the war effort to entrust these operations to workers who cannot read and write" (117: 178).

The Army program

When the June 1, 1943 directive stated the military would take all men who were able to pass an intelligence exam, the Army saw that remedial action was needed immediately. Special Training Units (STU) were created by the end of that month. The purpose of the units was to help illiterate personnel acquire academic abilities needed for army life. The units were staffed by enlisted personnel who had previous experience in teaching, although not necessarily in teaching adults. From time to time, conferences were held to aid teachers in using their materials and working with the program (*17*: 12).

The program operated in the following manner. Personnel discovered to be illiterate were given a battery of tests including psychological interviews, medical tests, and placement tests. Based on the results of this battery, the inductee was assigned to an appropriate group (*62*: 601).

Classes were kept small so a student would be able to progress quickly from one level to another. The typical beginning class had fifteen students, while more advanced classes had eighteen to twenty students. The class period was three hours long and classes met six days a week. The time was devoted mainly to reading, language, and arithmetic. The remainder of the day included study about topics related to army life. The length of the program varied from eight to thirteen weeks, depending on the enrollee. Once a student attained an ability to function at grade level four, he was placed in the regular training program. If, after thirteen weeks, a student was *not* able to assume regular training, he was discharged (*197*: 354).

Special materials for army illiterates

Not only was it necessary for Army personnel to take on the task of teaching illiterates, but it was soon apparent they would have to produce the materials needed to keep the program operational. This they did in abundance. The approach used in teaching these disadvantaged inductees was functional, and the skills and materials introduced were related to daily life in the service. All materials had dual purposes—to teach the illiterate to read, and to help him adjust to army life.

In preparing the instructional materials for illiterates, a word list was created by using a count of words from the soldier's manuals. In addition, special lists were compiled from various military subjects such as military discipline. These words then provided a stock vocabulary for filmstrips, texts, and workbooks (*196*: 271).

Instruction began with the use of a filmstrip to develop vocabulary. In this way the student's first experience with a text proved more successful. Initial reading vocabulary included mainly nouns and useful verbs. The filmstrips contained a series of frames designed to provide experience in contextual reading. Included in the titles were: *The Story of Private Pete, A Soldier's General Orders, Military Discipline and Courtesy, How to Wear Your Uniform, Introduction to Numbers,* and *The World.* Each filmstrip had an *Instructor's Reference* which provided the guidance for conducting the filmstrip lesson (*196:* 272).

There were a number of textbooks designed to follow the readiness filmstrips. The *Army Reader* was one of the original basic reading texts in the program and was designed to be used after the filmstrip, *The Story of Private Pete.* The filmstrip and text both dealt with a soldier's adjustment to army life (*197:* 388).

Men in Armed Forces, A Serviceman's Reader was another basic text used in the literacy classes. The book recorded the story of Private Pete and his decision to join the Army. Although it started at a very low level of readability, the introduction of vocabulary was rapid, with very little reinforcement in the 252 pages. The text had large type and contained black and white cartoon-like illustrations which occupied about half the page. Following each chapter was a series of comprehension questions (*209*).

Servicemen Learn to Read, Practice Books I and II complemented the work in *A Serviceman's Reader.* These workbooks were designed to develop word recognition skills and comprehension. For every story in *A Serviceman's Reader,* there was a series of exercises in the workbook. Instructions were read by the teacher until the student had progressed far enough to read them himself (*211*).

Still other supplementary materials were produced to help the student maintain and reinforce his reading skills. The material appeared in a variety of forms. *Your Job in the Army* was a booklet which described the various duties in the service and was illustrated with line drawings and photographs. *The Newsmap Supplement,* a low readability version of *The Newsmap,* was a one-sheet weekly which provided current news about the war front. *Our War,* an eight-page periodical published monthly, provided pleasure reading. The publication included cartoons, photographs, human interest items, and stories about current events. Like the other supplementary materials, it was written at a readability level of grade three (*197:* 388).

In addition to the aforementioned materials, a series of independent readers was developed. The readers were designed to be used without supervision. The stories continued to follow the theme of army life and were several pages long. The books contained no illustrations, and each story was followed by a skill lesson in alphabetizing, using vowel sounds, and correct language usage. Student answer keys were provided for self-evaluation. *Friends in Service* is an example of such an independent reader (*208*).

A small portion of the literacy program included instruction to develop arithmetic skills. The approach used was similar to that used in the reading instruction. A filmstrip, *Introduction to Numbers*, was used to provide background in number concepts. *Army Arithmetic*, the basic text, presented concepts and problems in an army setting (*197: 389*).

An appraisal of the program

The Army's venture into literacy training was described in detail by Goldberg (*22: 281-283*) in 1951. In his definitive record of this literacy program, he identified five special circumstances which help explain the success experienced by the Army.

Service personnel proved to be more highly motivated than their civilian counterparts since reading and writing provided a way to keep in touch with family during the war years. Because the soldier was under the control of the Army twenty-four hours a day, optimal times could be selected for instruction and reinforcement of skills. These lessons were conducted by highly qualified personnel and backed with unlimited funds for materials and instructional aids. Finally, the Army was free to develop techniques and materials without experiencing the repercussions of a conservative civilian population.

The program itself stressed a functional approach and utilized strong visual aids such as filmstrips, flashcards, pictures, posters, maps, cartoons, and models. The use of these aids, in conjunction with small classes and appropriate and relevant materials, helped account for the success of the program.

Witty and Van Buskirk (*201: 9*) reported that 60 to 95 percent of the inductees were saved for military service through the program. On still another occasion, Witty claimed that 90 percent of the men enrolled reached the fourth grade standard.

One critic cautioned that the actual percentages of success needed to be interpreted carefully. He pointed out that pressures on administrators encouraged them to have good records, even if they were only on paper. Since the Army records are the only ones available on the program, they would probably be considered less than scientific data (*62: 602*).

Whether the percentage of success was as high as Witty claimed is probably not the most important factor concerning the Army program. More important is the fact that the program was most likely the largest and most extensive program ever undertaken. Most assuredly, it was the best equipped.

The Navy program

During the years the Navy was composed of volunteer personnel, it had been possible to maintain high educational standards. But when the Selective Service poured thousands of illiterate individuals into this service, the Navy had to deal with a problem as serious as the Army's. The first attempt to solve this problem was the decision to assign the illiterates to nonreading jobs. Although the plan seemed sound, it was not long before it was discovered that few such jobs existed.

It was inevitable—the inductees had to be taught to read and write. Teachers were taken from the ranks, materials were created, and methods and techniques for adults were devised. In 1944 the Navywide literacy program officially started.

The program and texts of the Navy were very similar to those used by the Army. *The Navy Life Series* contained basic readers, workbooks, supplemental readers, tests, and teacher manuals. The first book to be introduced was the workbook. This was an attempt to force teachers away from round robin class reading (*173*: 203). Only after extensive chart, blackboard, and workbook experience was the first reader introduced. The student was then able to read for meaning immediately, since the book contained no new words. "As a result, the student is literate so far as the readers are concerned with his very first experience with them" (*173*: 204).

Comic books provided an extremely popular source of supplementary reading. Certain comics were selected as suitable in advance of the publication date. They were then rewritten for the students, using the stock vocabulary compiled by the Navy.

The arithmetic program, a small segment of the Navy's literacy program, was similar to that of the Army. The program stressed only what was of immediate use. It emphasized the basic processes using money as a basis.

The Selective Service asks for help

The number of illiterate registrants was so large that the National Selective Service Headquarters and the United States Office of Education requested state and local officials to cooperate with local Selective Service Boards in providing literacy classes for registrants.

Once literacy training centers had been established, registrants were assigned to a local center for educational assessment. The illiterates were then enrolled in classes. Local Selective Service Boards helped maintain attendance in the programs.

Unfortunately, no federal funds were available for such programs and state and local boards had to bear the expenses themselves. They had the satisfaction of knowing it would save the Army valuable training time later on. Although the government did not provide financial support for the program, it did provide a list of materials which could be used in classes (*143*: 15).

Many in the military felt it was the duty of civilian communities to help handle the problem. Lt. General Brehon Sommerville clearly stated: "The upgrading of the illiterate is a responsibility that the Army should not be compelled to assume at this time. We can spare neither the physical facilities nor the personnel" (*81*: 131).

Project for Adult Education of Negroes

Only one major civilian literacy effort appeared in the literature during the forties. In 1946, the American Association on Adult Education, the National Conference on Adult Education and the Negro, and the United States Office of Education undertook a project which aimed to "raise the educational level of a large number of Negroes whom the Selective Service and the 1940 census described as functionally illiterate" (*78*: 26). The main financing was from two grants presented by the Carnegie Corporation of New York. The funds totaled over $49,910 and were allotted for a total of three years (*276*: 1). Directing the project was Ambrose Cavalier, the USOE specialist for higher education of Negroes. The associate director was William Cooper, secretary-treasurer of the National Conference on Adult Education and the Negro.

After an organizational conference, an institute was held at Hampton Institute, Virginia, on September 14, 1946. Its purposes were:

1) to prepare personnel for the training and supervision of teachers of adults in the fundamental processes; 2) to demonstrate the effectiveness for civilian use of certain techniques developed by the Army; 3) to collect and evaluate resource materials for teaching of adults; 4) to identify and classify the major problems of Negroes that are amendable to adult education on the elementary level; and 5) to formulate a tentative curriculum and instructional guide on the elementary level for teachers of Negro adults (*78*: 27).

At the end of the project, a fair amount of progress had been made. Worth noting are the experimental materials which had been produced. A set of four basic readers included: *A Day with the Brown Family, Making a Good Living, The Browns at School,* and *The*

Browns and Their Neighbors. Workbooks in language, reading, and arithmetic were produced along with supplementary readers, a teacher guide, and syllabus for an introductory course for teachers of adults. Nearly 1,000 teachers of adults were exposed to new methods and techniques during the project (*79*: 74-75).

In February 1948 a final evaluation conference was held. At this conference it was noted that there appeared to be a renewed interest in literacy education. As evidence, it was pointed out that Miner Teachers College of Washington, D.C. conducted classes for teachers of adults with no financial aid for the program. In addition, divisions ten to thirteen of the public school system of Washington, D.C. conducted classes for illiterate adults. Similar classes were held in the public schools in Baltimore and Atlanta. Still other classes were initiated in Albany, Georgia and in Little Rock, Arkansas. State Departments of Education in Alabama, Arkansas, Georgia, Louisiana, Mississippi, South Carolina, and Texas began to show active interest in literacy education (*276*: 6).

The grant ended in 1948, but a skeleton staff was retained in order to prepare and revise materials and provide consultative services. The workers of the project felt they had psychologically paved the way for a nationwide campaign against illiteracy, but such a campaign would need the aid of the federal government.

Realistically viewing the problem, F.S. Chase stated: "If the federal government is really in earnest about improving the educational status of those millions of adults, it must be prepared to bear a large share of the cost of providing teachers and facilities" (*92*: 70). The years to come would reveal the extent of the federal government's concern.

Legislation

By the end of World War II, nearly three-quarters of a million persons had been rejected from the service because of educational deficiencies. These individuals were lost to defense and mobilization and would probably be lost to a profitable civilian life too (*81*: 131). Those who had been salvaged, at least temporarily, from illiteracy were returning to civilian life. A question remained: would these persons be urged on by society or lose what they had gained in an apathetic community?

The Office of Education reported in a survey that some states were beginning to broaden adult education to include elementary education for adults. In some instances, programs were given financial aid and supervision by the state.

At a national level, there was virtually no legislative progress. In

1948, and again in 1949, Senator Harley M. Kilgore of West Virginia introduced literacy bills in Congress. The bills proposed to financially assist states in removing illiteracy. Senator Kilgore emphasized the fact that a problem of such magnitude needed a coordinated and massive attack. He was unsuccessful in his endeavors (*140:* 90-91).

The only federal legislation significantly related to illiteracy appeared to be the Serviceman's Readjustment Act of 1944. According to Title 2,

> Any person who served in the active military or naval service on or after September 16, 1940, and prior to the termination of the present war, and who shall have discharged or released therefrom under conditions other than dishonorable, and whose education or training was impeded, delayed or interfered with by reason of his entrance into the service, or who desires a refresher or retraining course...shall be eligible for and entitled to receive education or training (*195:* 3).

Thus, there was still some hope that these new literates would qualify for benefits and retain their newly acquired skills. Although it was helpful, this legislation did not provide for the massive attack needed to alleviate the problem.

Witty stated that illiteracy did not have to exist in communities if they would provide equal educational opportunities, have compulsory schooling, extend opportunities to the adult level, and provide schools for illiterate adults (*195:* 3). Witty's points were well taken but there is little evidence that legal steps were taken to bring about the changes needed.

Summary

During the forties, the United States again became concerned with the thousands of illiterate registrants called for World War II. As a result, efforts along the literacy fronts were mainly in the form of military programs as the armed forces undertook to rapidly train these illiterates in the basic skills of reading and writing.

For the first time, there was an abundance of materials designed specifically for teaching adults. The materials were produced mainly for use in the military environment, however, and not for civilian life. These readers, workbooks, filmstrips, and magazines were the forerunners of civilian materials published some years later.

Since most efforts were being directed toward the war and war needs, little appears to have been done along professional lines. The only notable civilian effort during the period was the Project for

Adult Education of Negroes, sponsored by the Carnegie Corporation. As a result of the program, a number of instructional materials and teaching aids were produced, and approximately 1,000 teachers were trained in new methods and techniques of literacy education.

Although there were no really great contributions to literacy education during the forties, the war did create an awareness of the problem. Military leaders, political figures, and educators were begining to realize the task of educating the illiterate adult could not be left to the amateur and volunteer. Neither could it be left to chance and corrected if necessity required it. The forties, then, can be described as an incubation period for the ideas that would emerge concretely in the next twenty years.

Chapter Six

1950-1959: A Period of Adjustment

Social Climate

The period from 1950 to 1959 could probably be described as a period of adjustment for the United States. This adjustment occurred in all areas of major importance—the economy, foreign affairs, domestic policies, and education. Major issues could no longer be circumvented, and problems which had been incubating for years came to the surface during this decade.

International affairs

After World War II, tension between the United States and Russia became increasingly obvious in the "cold war" atmosphere. The United States, centering its foreign policy around support of the United Nations, tried to avoid any extensive commitments with foreign countries. But on June 25, 1950, Communist forces invaded South Korea. When the United Nations authorized the use of force to stop aggression, it was the United States that provided the greatest number of personnel for the international army. The struggle continued for several years.

The strain placed on the economy and manpower during this conflict closely resembled that of World War II. An armistice was signed in July 1953, but the only positive factor resulting was that the spread of Communism had been somewhat restrained. The conflict left the people of the United States with a radical interest in internal Communism and foreign countries became fearful of America's impulsive threats to Communists. As a result, American attitudes shifted slightly toward isolationism.

When Russia launched the first satellite in 1957, direction was given to the vacillating attitudes held by the United States. Political dangers made it necessary for the United States to keep ahead of Russia in her scientific developments. As a result, school curriculums were revised, greater financial support for science was provided, and a new emphasis was placed on academic achievement (*28*: 857-858).

The domestic scene

The American economic situation vacillated between good times and recession. There were more money, more leisure time, and more social benefits, but personal debt was higher and the farmer's income was dropping.

In the 1948 election Harry Truman carried a civil rights plank proposed by Hubert Humphrey. The plank guaranteed such basic and fundamental rights as equal opportunity of employment and equal treatment in the services and defense of our nation. The reform program also included federal aid to education, national health insurance, and extension of Social Security.

Truman defeated Dewey, but he did not secure the support of Congress. When his reform bill was presented, almost every major part was defeated. It took almost the entire decade before the American public finally realized the importance of these issues and acted accordingly (*28*: 843-845).

Interest in equal opportunities and social welfare legislation continued with the Eisenhower administration. A significant issue, which helped determine the direction in which the country was headed, was the Supreme Court decision concerning segregated schools. In May 1954, the Court made the following announcement: "We conclude that in the field of public education the doctrine of 'separate but equal' has no place. Separate educational facilities are inherently unequal" (*18*: 847). This statement was the first indication that a period of social reform would follow in the next decade.

An interest in education

During the early fifties there was some concern about education, but efforts to deal with problems indicated this area was also experiencing a period of change. There was a large influx of students into the schools and colleges. This rapid increase of students led to a shortage of teachers. As a result, one of the educational tasks of the time became the improvement of schools.

Progress was being made in other areas of education. In 1950, Congress established the National Science Foundation and, in 1953, the Department of Health, Education, and Welfare was formed with

Oveta Culp Hobby serving as Secretary. In May 1954, the case of Brown vs. Board of Education of Topeka resulted in the decision that separate educational facilities were inherently unequal. With this decision thousands of Southern schools started the long and difficult path toward desegregation (*18*: 851-853).

Perhaps the most outstanding event to influence education during the fifties was the launching of the Russian satellite in October 1957. A shocked America rapidly overhauled science curriculums and proposed greater financial support of academic achievement. With a single event, the importance of educating American citizens became abundantly clear. The adjustments made during the fifties provided the impetus for action in the sixties.

Motivation

There were probably several factors which motivated the literacy efforts of the fifties. Although no major federal legislation supported an adult literacy education program, there was an increasing awareness of the need for a basic education in an expanding industrial society. Individuals who were unable to read and write could not hope to survive in such a society without some type of help.

It also became apparent during this time that there were large numbers of people who were not afforded the same economic and educational opportunities enjoyed by the majority of citizens. It was necessary to provide these people, adults and children alike, the opportunities that were rightfully theirs.

The expanding sphere of Communism also motivated interest in educating citizens. In order to evaluate propaganda, it was necessary to have an intelligent populus. The need for education was further emphasized when the Russian satellite was launched. It was then necessary for the educational systems of the United States to keep pace with or surpass Russia, so the country might maintain its position of power.

As a final stimulus for literacy action, there was the Korean conflict. After four decades, the illiterate soldier was still a problem to the military. The statistics dealing with illiterate soldiers varied little, but the demands for literacy became ever increasing as wars became more mechanized. Stimulated directly or indirectly by these factors, the wheels of progress for literacy education slowly started to turn during the fifties.

The Statistics

The 1950 census

The 1950 census followed the precedent set by the 1940 census when information on grade completion was provided in lieu of illiteracy statistics. While this form of literacy data was available in the 1940 census for individuals between the ages of ten and fourteen, no such data were included in the 1950 census. Instead, fourteen was used as a base age. This change was probably influenced most by the fact that many compulsory school laws would not allow a child to terminate his education before age fourteen.

In 1950, illiteracy was defined as "the inability to read and write either in English or in any other language" (227: 1). Using that definition, it was "estimated that the number of illiterates 14 years and over in 1950 was about 3,600,000 or 3.2 percent of the corresponding population" (219: 47). This indicated a drop of 1.0 percent from the previous decade. It should be noted that, although this information was reported in the census, the final statistic was an estimate which resulted from two surveys on illiteracy conducted in 1947 and 1952 (219: 47). No actual count of illiterates was taken in the 1950 census. Since the total of individuals in the no-schooling group closely resembled the total cited as illiterate, the given estimates were considered fairly accurate.

The 1950 census provided information concerning grade completion but did not define the term "functional illiterate." Therefore, during this decade, one must assume the federal government continued to use the definition formulated in the forties. As the reader will recall, a functional illiterate was one who had completed less than five years of elementary school. This does not imply, however, the individual has *completed* four years of school (233: 3). Since the definition for illiteracy was based on age fourteen, one can assume the same held true for functional illiterates. In 1950 there were 10,481,320 individuals who had no schooling, or who had completed less than five years of school. In the previous decade, there were over a million more individuals who were classified as functional illiterates and they amounted to 11.6 percent of the population (239).

In many instances, statistics concerning functional illiterates were provided using a base age of twenty-five. There did not appear to be any particular reason for the use of this base age, but the figures connected with it were revealing. Viewing the problem as a whole, one discovers these functionally illiterate adults totaled 11 percent of the population (76: 191). Indeed, there were at least seven states whose percentage of functionally illiterate adults greatly exceeded the national average. Over 25 percent of the population in Louisiana, South Carolina, and Mississippi were functionally illiterate. This problem was not confined to the Southern states alone. Even states with lower percentages faced overwhelming numbers of functional illiterates. New York claimed 900,000; Pennsylvania, over 500,000; and California and Illinois, 400,000 (*248*: 5-9).

Although the figures for functional illiterates were high, the percentage of absolute illiterates was more encouraging. The decline in this figure was probably the result of population changes. One such factor may have been the migration from rural areas to cities (*236*: 6). Illiteracy rates for farm population had always been higher than for nonfarm population. This was probably because schools in rural areas were few and often inaccessible. The migration at midcentury brought a great many people to the urban areas where educational opportunities were available. Those that remained behind were often the less literate; but improved roads, public transportation, and school consolidation eventually made it possible for these rural people to receive an adequate education (*76*: 194).

Another factor influencing the illiteracy statistics was more schooling. Data collected by the Bureau of Census indicated a pattern of increasing educational attainment at younger ages. For those in the age group of sixty-five and over, the median grade completed was 8.2. The subjects in the age group forty-five to fifty-four had completed an average of 9.0 grades, while those twenty-five to thirty-four were high school graduates, with the median grade of 12.2. This trend appeared reasonable since, as persons pass on to older age groups or die, they are followed by those with more education. Also, as great waves of immigration passed and the people were assimilated, their influence on illiteracy statistics became less and less (*236*: 4).

The 1959 survey

From time to time, the Bureau of Census conducted population surveys on literacy and educational attainment. The studies were extremely useful since no literacy questions had been asked on the census since 1930. These surveys provided the figures needed to estimate illiteracy rates each decade. Such a study was conducted in 1959.

In this survey, there was a change in the definition of illiteracy. It was the first variation since the term was redefined in 1930. In this survey, illiteracy was defined as "the inability to read and write a simple message in English or in any other language" (*234*: 9). According to the definition, about 2.2 percent of the people over the age of fourteen were estimated to be illiterate. The bureau commented: "This is the smallest percentage of illiterates ever recorded in this country and represents a continuation of the historic decline in the inability to read and write" (*234:* 1). The steady decline was represented in still another manner. In 1870, the percentage of white illiterates was 12.0, and in 1959 it had dropped to an estimated 2.0 percent. The drop for nonwhites was a much more striking one—from 80.0 percent in 1870 to 8.0 percent in 1959. The report also noted that the rate of illiteracy for native whites was probably nearing its minimum point. It indicated that a great proportion of these remaining illiterates were probably unable to learn to read and write because of physical or mental deficiencies.

Similar to past trends, the survey reported illiteracy rates were higher for older age groups, the unemployed, farm and nonagricultural laborers, and in areas of the South. A continuing uptrend in educational attainment was also evident (*234:* 1-2).

The extremely low rate of illiteracy was probably influenced by several factors related to the survey: 1) the data were subject to sampling error and the experience of the enumerator, 2) the survey did not include those in the armed services or institutions, and 3) those foreign born who could barely function with literacy skills could be counted as literate according to the definition. These factors may account for the slight difference in illiteracy rates which appear in the 1960 census.

Legislation

Although the fifties was an active decade in terms of educational legislation, there was no federal legislation passed which related to literacy education. Programs appeared to have been implemented mainly by state laws and local ordinances. In many instances, this legislation had been passed prior to the fifties.

Programs expanded slowly, but by 1959 every state, except Kansas, had provided legislation pertaining to general adult education. Holden described the adult education services of the State Education Departments in the late fifties. At that time seven states made elementary grade classes, including classes for illiterates, mandatory under given conditions. These states included California, Connecticut, Massachusetts, New Hampshire, Pennsylvania, Rhode Island, and Utah. With the exception of Utah, state aid was authorized to finance these programs.

Four states had permissive legislation with some qualifications or restrictions. Colorado and Idaho had legislation which stated that local districts could establish classes in first-class cities or districts. In Georgia, programs could be established for persons between fourteen and thirty if they were unable to attend day school.

Kansas, Kentucky, Missouri, Oklahoma, and South Dakota had

no legal provisions for elementary grade classes, while the remaining thirty-two states had permissive legislation.

The methods of financing these programs varied greatly. In some instances, they were privately financed utilizing tuition, fees, and contributions, but no state or local tax funds. In other instances, the programs were locally financed with tax funds. Finally, state aid might be authorized in order to supplement local, private, or public funds. Although states may have authorized state aid, it did not necessarily mean that the money was appropriated. This, of course, limited the number of literacy classes that might exist (*241*).

Programs

Illiteracy and national defense

When the Communist forces invaded South Korea in 1950 the draft calls began to increase, but during the first year of the conflict about 500,000 men were rejected for service. This was equivalent to about 35 percent of those men examined. Approximately 300,000 men were rejected for educational deficiencies, with the greatest rejection rates being for those from the South (*248*: 4). The highest percentage of Selective Service rejections on the Armed Forces Qualifications Test was 58 percent from South Carolina, while the national rejection rate for this period was 19.2 percent (*167*: 136). Figures from Korea and Washington, D.C. also revealed that 10 to 15 percent of the enlisted men entering the Army during the Korean War had less than a fourth grade training (*74*: 171).

The problem appeared to be the result of substandard educational facilities. As a result, thousands of men from states with higher standards had to be drafted in order to make up the deficiency in manpower. It was here, some argued, that equalization with federal aid would equalize the draft burden (*150*: 35). Roy K. Davenport, of the Adjutant General's Office, Department of the Army, made this comment: "If educational opportunities in all areas for both races had been identical, nearly all of the sectional and racial differences would disappear" (*141*: 4).

The need for the "lost men" was further emphasized in January 1951 when President Truman indicated that the "primary aim of our manpower mobilization is to safeguard our national security through maximum development and use of our natural resources" (*81*: 131). In order to make this effective, it was necessary to have a literate population since illiteracy was one of the main problems in manpower mobilization. "While illiterates are at a disadvantage in civilian life, they may be a distinct hazard in a military situation"

(*119*: 31).

To further investigate this condition a private organization, the Human Resources Research Office (HumRRO), conducted a study of marginal troops during the Korean emergency. Their findings revealed that 1) since the weapons being used were capable of greater fire power, greater brainpower was needed to operate them; 2) marginal soldiers proved to be a source of danger to good soldiers; and 3) the combat soldier who was a good fighter usually had more education and potential than the nonfighter. HumRRO stated that "to the extent that the Army is forced to accept men from the national manpower pool who are low in ability, to such an extent will its fighting potential be reduced" (*184*: 66).

Although the military was deeply involved in the problem of illiteracy, this was not by choice. It was the general opinion of those in the service, and many educators, that the responsibility of educating these men belonged to local communities and the states. In addition, many felt both were often quite negligent in assuming these duties. Ambrose Caliver of the U.S. Office of Education stated:

> Much of our adult illiteracy exists in states that find difficulty in supporting an adequate program of education for children and youth. In fact, there is considerable (negative) relationship between the level of support of general education in a State and the number of functionally illiterate adults in the State (*81*: 132).

As one writer expressed it:

> Yesterday, illiteracy was merely a national disgrace. Today, in the face of the Communist threat, illiteracy is a grave national problem. Tomorrow, if our states and communities do not take steps to abolish it, illiteracy can be a national disaster (*184*: 67).

The Armed Services and illiterates

The Selective Service Act provided that men could not be rejected for mental deficiency if they attained the minimal score on a screening test, but the score established by Congress was quite minimal. It permitted many low ability recruits to enter the service and this was particularly true in the Army. In order to remedy the situation, Secretary of Defense James Forrestal issued a directive which called for an equal division of recruits among the services. This division was based on mental fitness. The plan had loopholes, however, and the Air Force and the Navy still acquired more of the brighter inductees (*184*: 23).

Although the minimal score on the screening test was considered very low, Southern Congresspersons claimed it was high enough to call all whites and reject the blacks. So, as a result of the pressures from the Southern members of Congress, the minimal score was lowered further in 1950. The resulting score was equivalent to the lowest score accepted during World War II (*184:* 24).

Consequently, the Armed Forces once again found themselves saddled with illiterates and forced to undertake the burden of their literacy training. The Army defined an illiterate as one who was not able to read and write "the English language as commonly prescribed for the fourth grade in grammar school" (*172:* 440). Thus, the Army literacy programs aspired to that level of training.

In order to utilize the low ability manpower, the Army established special schools in 1949. Between 1949 and 1954 they reported 257,000 illiterates were brought to a performance level of grade five. Early in 1954 these schools were reorganized, and seven transitional training units were established. Marginal draftees who were sent to these units received training in the basic literacy skills and were exposed to limited military training (*184:* 24).

Although the Army did provide the means to train the undereducated men, it was displeased with the task. Army reports estimated that over a two-year period, approximately 10.8 percent of the inductees needed literacy training (*172:* 440). Even after these inductees were trained, a problem remained. The draftees served only two years in the service, and seven to eight months were needed for literacy training. Thus, the recruit was useful for only sixteen or seventeen months. In addition to the cost of time, the situation of using low ability personnel proved costly in terms of discipline and morale (*184:* 24). One must conclude that the Army performed its task out of necessity and at the price of time, equipment, personnel, and efficiency.

The Navy was also faced with schooling undereducated persons as illiterates filtered into that service. In an attempt to deal with their share of marginal individuals, the Navy established a literacy training program which preceded regular indoctrination. Special training units were located at Bainbridge, Maryland; Great Lakes, Illinois; and San Diego, California. These units, officially called Recruit Preparatory Training Units, provided a maximum of thirteen weeks literacy training before sending the recruit on to basic training.

In both the Army and Navy programs, instruction was designed to deal with service life. Classes were small and staffed by volunteers, and students were allowed to progress at their own rates. The materials used were similar to the ones used in World War II training. Readers, workbooks, and instructors' guides provided the basic instruction. Maps, charts, flash cards, and signs were often used to supplement lessons. The main purpose of these materials was to prepare men to be soldiers as quickly as possible.

Coach classes

As the demands of society change, it becomes increasingly difficult to establish the criteria used to measure illiteracy. With each decade, the populus needs to be more literate. It is our belief that a democratic society can exist only with an informed public. Perhaps it was fear for the society that motivated some major civilian literacy programs during the fifties, or it may have been an awareness created by the Korean War figures.

As early as 1839 the Department of Education of Baltimore, Maryland, was concerned with providing adults with the basic tools of learning, and conducted evening schools to help alleviate the problem. In 1950, Baltimore alone had 22,055 persons twenty-five and older who did not have fundamental skills.

The Baltimore programs of the fifties were designed to meet the immediate needs and interests of adults. These coach classes provided adults with practical experience in filling out work forms, reading signs on the job, and forming shopping lists. The cooperation of libraries, museums, social groups, labor, and schools was requested in order to supplement the program.

The program emphasized the use of materials written at an adult level of interest with low readability. The individuals were allowed to progress at their own pace to assure success and self-confidence (*170:* 37-41).

A new media for illiterates

Although most literacy programs followed a format similar to that used in Baltimore, there was one very significant change which took place in 1957. It was at this time that Keith Nighbert, a program director at WKNO TV in Memphis, initiated the use of television as an instructional medium for illiterates.

Nighbert became interested in the Laubach method of teaching illiterates and saw the possibilities of adapting this approach for television. Once he received the approval of Frank Laubach, a program was initiated for the 57,000 adult illiterates in the Memphis area.

The program was designed to bring illiterates through grade level four. It was estimated that 350 hours would be needed to achieve this goal. The 350 hours included half-hour television lessons three times a week, and homework supervised by volunteers in the viewing centers. Thirty-four of these television reading centers were established by the time the program was ready to begin.

At the end of two years, a program report estimated that approximately 2,000 adults had been brought to a level of functional literacy. This indicated the programs had reached successfully only 3 percent of the potential public during this period. Several other factors were indicators of the questionable success of the program. First, it was discovered that adults were very impatient about the learning process; they dropped by the wayside if the pace was too slow. A faster pace often resulted in the lack of proper reinforcement or discouraged students. Also, learning slowed down when there was a gap of more than forty-eight hours between instructional periods. Even though the program was not very successful, many requests were made to obtain the lessons. WKNO TV packaged ninety-eight half-hour lessons and sold them to interested television stations (*185*).

Illiteracy in the prisons

When we think of illiterates and functional illiterates, we often fail to remember the large number of these people in various institutions. In fact, in many illiteracy counts these people have actually been eliminated from the tally. Illiterates are present in institutions and, in many instances, some feeble attempt is made to educate them.

D'Amico and Strandlee conducted an investigation on this topic. Responses from 112 state prisons, representing 43 states and 14 federal institutions, yielded the following information. In most instances, prisoners were given an orientation talk by the educational specialist or psychologist. The basic theme of the speech usually included the advantages of being able to read and write. Shortly afterward the prisoners were given an educational achievement test. The Stanford Achievement Test was the one used most frequently in these institutions.

Based on the results of the exam, anyone achieving less than grade five was compelled to attend school to that level. In some states the law required an eighth grade level of achievement. In most cases, classes were conducted by inmates, although civilian teachers were used occasionally.

It was reported that over 156 different materials were used for instruction. These included filmstrips, flash cards, and word games, but all institutions reported the need for materials which appealed to adults. The investigators concluded that in most instances operating budgets were too small, libraries inadequate, and facilities and equipment were poor. The study seemed to reveal that if literacy programs were inadequate in civilian life they were even more inadequate in institutions (*105*:218).

Industry's interest in illiteracy

During the early years of the twentieth century, industry became interested in illiteracy in relationship to the large number of foreign-born employed. Although often motivated by less than noble reasons, literacy programs were occasionally started for these employees. As the years passed, the number of non-English speaking employees decreased, general illiteracy rates dropped, and the prevalence of illiteracy in American industry diminished.

It diminished, but it did not disappear. In the fifties, the Bureau of Census reported the educational level of workers was 11.0 years. This appeared very impressive. The Bureau also noted that 6.8 percent of the working force had less than five years of schooling. Therefore, 6.8 percent of the working force were considered functionally illiterate. Approximately 2.0 percent of all workers were unable to read and write in any language. For nonwhite workers, the illiteracy rate was 10.0 percent. These figures indicated that illiteracy was still a problem in industry (*223*:1-14).

Investigating the educational programs conducted by industry, Clark and Sloan reported on 349 of America's leading corporations. Size of each corporation was determined by the amount of dollar sales. The results were interesting because of what they failed to say about literacy education. Only forty-seven corporations conducted programs in general education. Elementary School Subjects was one of nineteen classifications under general education, with Reading one of six subdivisions. It was fairly obvious that literacy training was viewed as relatively unimportant in total scope of industry's educational programs (*16*).

The writer discovered only one report during the fifties concerning an actual program sponsored by industry. In East Baton Rouge Parish, Louisiana, Esso Standard Oil Company asked the public school literacy department to take on 1,450 workers for literacy training and Esso provided the $1,000 per month needed to support the program.

Since no follow-up reports were available, it is not clear how successful the program was or whether it continued. Surely this lack of literature indicates that industry's concern for the illiterate was not very extensive during the fifties (*165*:68).

Professional Activities

During the fifties, the American public's concern for education began to filter down to literacy education. It was during this decade that some of the first professional programs, materials, and studies appeared. In 1951, at a UNESCO conference held in Geneva, Switzerland, forty-three nations pledged to devote their efforts toward free compulsory education. The United States pledged itself to further extend the educational opportunities to even higher age groups (*149*:106).

In 1952, the Adult Education Association of the United States set up a committee on Adult and Fundamental Education. It was the purpose of this committee to investigate problems in this area. In 1955, the Office of Education established an Adult Education Section for a similar purpose (*85*:6).

Teacher training

One problem frequently encountered in literacy education was poor quality instructors. Very little had been done to train volunteers or prepare professional literacy teachers. This problem was approached in several ways.

One unique program was developed in 1952 at Syracuse University's School of Journalism. Since the lack of suitable adult literacy materials had long been an obvious problem, this program made it possible to train the writers needed to produce such materials (*100*:291).

Dealing with another aspect of professional training in literacy education, Baylor University Literacy Center developed a system to prepare volunteer teachers. In order to train these literacy leaders, the center conducted literacy workshops in Waco and Abilene, Texas and Clovis, New Mexico. The workshops usually lasted two days, with an evening session the first day and a half-day session the next. The programs were conducted by staff members from Baylor University Literacy Center.

A typical workshop usually included a demonstration of literacy materials, suggestions for contacting illiterates, topics for teacher-made materials, and suggestions for organizing local literacy councils. The workshops resulted in several literacy classes being organized and a Literacy Projects Board being established in each of the towns.

Although the workshop concept appeared successful, it was not widespread enough to noticeably affect the illiteracy situation. There were probably other similar efforts taking place during this period, but records of these appear to be nonexistent (*102*:54-56).

Still another facet of literacy education was training the professional literacy teacher. It was Baylor University, once again, that took the lead in establishing the first undergraduate curriculum in literacy education. The program basically followed this format:

Course One. This was a basic course which included the study of literacy methods, clinical practice, preparation of a literacy primer, use of literacy information supplied by the government and private agencies, and the investigation of the literacy problem and its implications.

Course Two. Emphasis in this course was placed on preparing literature for use with illiterates. In doing this, students acquired the skill needed to use reading formulae and participated in the Writers Guild for New Literates.

Course Three. This course was designed as an introduction to linguistics. It provided the student with an opportunity to study phonemics, phonetics, and morphology. The course of study included a survey of the languages of the world and techniques in teaching and learning foreign languages and also provided practice with the tape recorder and audiovisual equipment as it applied to language teaching.

Course Four. This course, which was optional in the program, dealt with teaching English as a foreign language.

In addition to traditional coursework, students were required to take part in local literacy councils and actually teach illiterates. They also assisted in organizing literacy programs and were apprentice trainers in the workshops held by Baylor Literacy Center. The program was designed to give the future teacher experience in many areas of literacy education (*100*:290-293).

National Commission for Adult Literacy

It is not an uncommon practice to establish a committee or commission to investigate severe problems which exist in our country. Most often it is the government which establishes the commission, but in some instances professional organizations having an immediate interest in the problem take on this task.

The National Commission for Adult Literacy was such a nongovernmental agency. It was established in 1957 by the Adult Education Association of the United States. The main purpose of this body was to stimulate all three levels of government "to give every adult an opportunity to acquire the basic skills of reading, writing, and arithmetic" (*80*:13).

It was the opinion of the commission that only a nationwide effort could help solve the problem of illiteracy. This group hoped to spark that interest. Under the leadership of Murry D. Lincoln and Paul A.

Witty, the commission was promotional, not operational in nature. The commission alerted the public to the need of dealing with illiteracy, collected illiteracy data, stimulated research and pilot programs, and initiated action through conferences and publications.

A financial campaign to raise a $450,000 budget was initiated in 1958. The commission located in Washington, D. C. and spent the next three years working toward its goals (*80*:13-14).

Methods and Materials

The Laubach Method was one approach to literacy instruction which became popular during the fifties. In many instances this method was adapted for television presentation.

Initial instruction began by introducing the student to an alphabet in which pictures were associated with the individual letters to help build strong associations. Special symbols were used to make the spelling of words more phonetic. The approach made use of a limited number of specially prepared materials, usually in the form of charts or workbooks accompanied by a teacher manual.

Since the workbook took the student through only the early stages of literacy, many supplementary materials were needed to round out the program. For the same reason, the method was often used in conjunction with experience stories (*36*).

Materials

The market for adult literacy materials during the fifties was little more than it had been during the previous decade. Often, teachers used materials designed for children and adapted them for adult classes. Success did not always follow. A study conducted by Kempfer in 1950 came to a similar conclusion. After surveying librarians and evening school principals, he concluded that the elementary level materials for adults were inadequate in number and topics (*65*: 218).

A few materials began to appear on the market, but the list was still scanty. Bibliographies (*348*) cited the following as some of the more appropriate materials produced during the decade.

How We Live. This hard cover book was designed to be used with beginning readers and those who were semiliterate. Sentences and paragraphs were short and simple and exercises followed each selection.

Rochester Occupational Reading Series. This series contained five books each dealing with one of the following topics: truck farms, bakeries, restaurants, supermarkets, and gas stations. Each of the books was written at three levels of readability. Level one was approximately third grade difficulty, level two was fourth grade, and level three was fifth. The series was suitable as a supplementary part of a program.

Achieving Reading Skills. The book presented reading skills on several levels of readability, progressing from grade level three to about grade level six.

How to Find a Job. This booklet was written at about readability level four. It discussed topics pertaining to finding a job, and included appropriate pictures and illustrations.

New Avenues in Reading. This book was written at about level four and was a combination reader and workbook. Comprehension and vocabulary exercises followed the selections. Written in a similar format, but at a higher level, were companion books — *New Journeys in Reading* and *New Adventures in Reading.*

Adult Reader. This was a supplementary book with a readability level of approximately grade two. The contents were topics of adult interest.

News For You. This was a unique newspaper written at three readability levels: two to three, three to four, and four to five. It was produced weekly and was the only one of its kind in the nation.

New Flights in Reading. Written at an intermediate level, this book contained a collection of stories and articles. Written exercises were included after each selection.

Men in the Armed Forces. This book was designed to be used as a supplement in a program. It ranged from readability level one through level four and was of high adult interest level.

Summary

The decade of the fifties was a period of adjustment in many phases of American life. The United States was initially involved in a cold war with Communist forces and later in actual military action. The economic situation vacillated between good times and recessions, and the country was troubled with fear of internal Communism. It was also a period of adjustment educationally. A Supreme Court decision declared separate educational facilities unequal, and the difficult task of desegregation began. Interest in science and school curriculums was stimulated in 1957 when the Russians launched the first satellite.

The statistics for illiteracy were lower in 1950 than ever before, but a new problem had arisen. By midcentury, the early definitions for literacy were no longer suitable and the term *functional illiterate* came into use. Though the percentage of illiterates had dropped, the number of people who could not function in society had increased, and might well continue to increase as educational demands became greater. The draft calls during the Korean encounter confirmed this fact.

By the late fifties most states had laws pertaining to adult elementary education, but there was no federal legislation to coordinate efforts. Programs were still being conducted at the local and state levels. In Memphis, Tennessee, an attempt was made to teach illiterates by using televised lessons. The project made use of the Laubach Method, an approach which gained popularity at the time.

Professional progress was made at Baylor University when a program was designed to train literacy volunteers. Baylor also created the first undergraduate curriculum for literacy specialists. At Syracuse University a curriculum was designed for training students in literacy journalism.

Finally, in an attempt to create interest in the problem and produce action, the National Commission for Adult Literacy was created. It was the hope of this body that governments at all levels would help solve the illiteracy problem. Just how effective this organization was would be evident in the sixties.

Chapter Seven

1960-1969: A Decade of Revolution

Social Climate

The new frontier

With the election of John F. Kennedy in 1960, attention was focused on the new problems of the day: pollution, materialism, a slowing economy, and neglect of the poor and old. It was Kennedy who initially stimulated the critical appraisal and social criticism of the sixties and also some of the answers for a partial solution.

The desire to cement good international relations for the future took on various social characteristics. The Peace Corps provided contact on an individual basis with those from underdeveloped countries. A Food for Peace program provided surplus American food for the same type of underdeveloped countries and the Alliance for Progress aimed to help Latin American countries develop economically, raise living standards, and provide opportunities for citizens.

When Kennedy entered office, the country was experiencing an economic recession. As a countermeasure, Kennedy pursued an expansionist policy and fought for tax reduction. As a result, there were increased output and employment, but a serious poverty situation still existed. Key poverty bills, such as federal aid to education and medical care for the aged, were defeated but many important advances were made including an increase in minimum wages, more liberal social security benefits, programs for economically distressed areas, and an omnibus housing bill.

The black revolution, receiving its initial impetus in the fifties, expanded rapidly during this period. Attention was directed toward poverty and injustices. Thirteen years after the Supreme Court decision on segregation, only 16 percent of the black students were attending desegregated schools. The youth, particularly impatient about prejudice, injustice, and poor education, turned to more radical leaders and organizations. These groups often favored violence, black power, and militant action, and riots in large and small cities became common news items (12: 831).

It was also the young people who expressed a deep concern about a growing situation in Vietnam. In the earliest days of the conflict, only military advisors were sent to Vietnam. In 1965, American military troops were sent in to reinforce the Vietnamese army. By 1967, American troops in Vietnam numbered half a million. "Each new step in escalation was accompanied by official predictions that it would reverse the tide of war" (12:826). Vietnam soon became a major issue of conflict in foreign policy.

A new administration

The 1968 presidential election brought Republican Richard Nixon to the White House. With his office, he inherited the task of ending an unpopular war, reducing the tension between the youth of America and the older establishment, and rectifying the social injustices of past generations.

The Statistics

The definition of illiterate

It has been observed by this writer that in the literature for the sixties, fewer references were made about "the illiterate" and more emphasis was placed on the concept of "functional illiteracy."

If it was difficult in the past to find a uniform and consistent definition for illiteracy, one finds even more difficult the task of defining functional illiteracy in the sixties. The range of possibilities became so great, one might often question if the same topic was being discussed.

Functional illiteracy was defined as, "all persons eighteen years or older who are unable to function above the third grade level in the areas of oral and written communication" (176:216). A second definition used in the sixties was "an adult twenty-five years of age or older who has had less than five years of formal education" (67:47). Fox viewed an illiterate as "that individual who does not have the necessary reading skills to make him eligible for vocational training when his marginal job in the labor market is discontinued" (120:7).

All of the sample definitions have some merit, whether it is the flexibility of the statement or its specificity in terms of age or functional level. Yet, it is these same factors which eventually cause limitations.

The definition needs to be flexible enough to be useful even when economic and social conditions have changed enough to make new and unique demands on the individual. Fox presented her ideas in this manner allowing for consistency in historical terms. Yet, one is unable to collect and itemize statistical data with so vague a definition. This, then, demonstrates the need for a complement definition using specifics.

Without an established basic age for "an adult," comparison of statistics is often of little value and may have no meaning. As noted in earlier chapters, an adult may range in age from ten to twenty-five, and studies using such a wide range are difficult, if not impossible, to analyze.

The problem arises, then, as to what basic age should be established. One might well suggest age eighteen as a reasonable possibility. Many compulsory school laws hold an individual off the job market and in school until almost that age. As a result, the greater portion of students continue their education until the completion of the high school program. This event usually takes place around age eighteen. It is approximately at this age, then, that the student makes a decision for further schooling or to terminate schooling and enter the working world.

A second reason for selecting this particular age is that legislation has extended the franchise to eighteen-year-olds in national elections.

Finally, many of the Adult Basic Education programs, arising from legislation such as the Economic Opportunity Act, establish age eighteen as a lower cut-off point for participants. These initial education and reeducation projects view an eighteen-year-old as an adult qualifying for benefits.

Once an age level for an adult has been established, a level of competency has to be determined. Because of the complexity of the society in which we live, the demands on the individual become increasingly intense. The skills one needs to survive are complex and varied in nature, and demand more education to acquire them. Thus, the level selected must provide one with enough background to progress through life in a comfortable manner. It is no longer reasonable to assume a fourth grade education is adequate to achieve this end. In fact, William S. Gray predicted that reading specialists would be dealing with a semiliterate at the seventh or eighth grade level of achievement (*100*:290).

Publications indicate that the United States Office of Education considered eight years of schooling a minimum for adequate comprehension and communication (*187*:3). It is probably worthwhile to note at this point that the term "eighth grade level of achievement" should be used and not the "completion of eighth grade" or "eighth grade education." Studies, such as the one conducted in the Woodlawn area of Chicago, clearly indicate that completion of a given grade does not mean an individual is performing at that level (*130*:1038).

Since it is impossible to administer achievement tests to the general population when national or state figures are the goal, a researcher is often left no choice but to use grade completion as a criterion. He should be well aware, however, that the figures he collects and the actual percentages dealing with illiteracy may differ drastically.

The 1960 census

Armed with this knowledge concerning age, level of achievement, and grade completion, one can now view the condition of the sixties. As in the two previous censuses, the 1960 census asked no literacy question per se. Nowhere in the census was illiteracy or functional illiteracy even defined. Data were included, however, on the number of individuals completing a given grade. So, when authors quote the 1960 census, they are using figures for grade completion and not percentages resulting from a specific literacy question. The writer is then able to manipulate these numbers for or against a cause merely by changing his definition of illiteracy. In some instances, accidental discrepancies may result when secondary sources do not define well enough. In other situations, the figures are meant to be misleading.

Initial inspection of the 1960 census revealed a general improvement in the educational status of the population. Only 18 percent of those seventy-five years and older had completed high school, while 64 percent of the twenty-year-olds had completed high school (*239*:xix).

If we describe an illiterate adult as one who has had no schooling, then 1.9 percent of those fourteen years of age and over were illiterate in this country. Using a base age of twenty-five, the percent increases to 2.3 percent of that population aged twenty-five and over. In both cases these figures indicate a slight drop of 0.3 percent from the 1950 census where the equivalent definitions produced the following results. For a population of fourteen years and over, 2.2 percent were illiterate; for a population twenty-five years and older, the figure was 2.6. In spite of the drop in percent, the actual number of illiterates increased (*239:* I-421).

As stated earlier in this section, concern should be focused on the functional illiterate as much as on the total illiterate. For this reason, the following figures may have much more significance in terms of representing the true size of the problem. If we use a definition for functional illiterate which was reasonable during the fifties and hold it consistent for the sixties, one may be able to view what progress, if any, had been made. The literature revealed that most definitions during the fifties established level five as the functional literacy level. Therefore, anyone completing less than five years of school could be classified as functionally illiterate. Included in these figures would be those individuals who had no schooling at all.

In 1950, approximately 10.5 million individuals age fourteen and older had less than a fifth grade education. This represented 9.6 percent of that population. In 1960, the figure dropped to approximately 8.9 million or 7.0 percent. When the basic age is changed to twenty-five, the corresponding results look like this. In 1950, about 9.5 million individuals were functionally illiterate, representing 11.1 percent of the population. In 1960, there was a drop to approximately 8 million people or 8.3 percent (239). At first glance, this indicated a sizable improvement of 2.8 percent. But by 1960, a fifth grade education was probably not considered adequate for complete participation in our society. Viewing the problem at a different level, approximately 20 million people fourteen years and over had less than seven years of schooling. This figure dropped to about 17.5 million for groups twenty-five years and older (239:407).

If one decided to analyze the 1960 data in terms of the more recent concepts of functional illiteracy, he would find that approximately 23 million people eighteen years and older had less than an eighth grade education. The figure dropped to 22 million for those twenty-five years and older (239:404). Remember, however, that this included those with no schooling or only a year as well as those with four, five, six, or seven years of education.

Thus, the picture was still grim. Percentages may appear to have dropped but, in actuality, millions of Americans were handicapped to such an extent that in the sixties the federal government finally took some concrete measures to help remedy the problem.

Legislation

At no other period in the history of adult literacy education has the federal government taken such an active interest in the problem of illiteracy as it did in the sixties. For the first time, concern expressed itself in the form of legislation, programs, and funds as opposed to solely moral support of the problem.

The constructive steps taken did not come about, however, without some failures. The Adult Literacy Bill introduced in the House of Representatives in 1962 died in the Rules Committee because of the opposition of Judge Howard Smith who headed the committee. In 1963, the bill again failed to get out of committee, but significant progress did start early in the sixties in spite of this initial failure (*158*:209).

Manpower Development and Training Act of 1962

The Manpower Development and Training Act (MDTA) of 1962 formed a partnership between the Department of Health, Education, and Welfare and the Department of Labor. Funds were appropriated to public and private agencies such as universities and industries which designed and carried out the MDTA program. Usually a survey was made of the industrial needs of the area, a curriculum was designed, and an educational program was set up. The programs aimed to provide further schooling for those unemployed youth and adults ages seventeen to twenty-one, in an effort to prepare them for vocational positions available in the area (*157*: 844). However, in Connecticut, ninety-seven out of one hundred selected for an MDTA program were unable to complete the program. In West Virginia, 50 percent of the people could not be retrained because they lacked *basic* skills (*190*:49).

Since many of the unemployed were functionally illiterate, an amendment to the act provided for adult basic education for those without enough educational skills to profit from the training (*157*:844). The act placed no limit on time for training, but payments to a trainee could not exceed seventy-two weeks. A youth could receive $20 per week while an adult received $10 per week over his regular unemployment compensation. A great deal of variety existed in the programs in terms of length of training time, type of training, and the manner in which the program was conducted.

Program support was continued through the Manpower Act of 1965. In this act, the training period was extended to 104 weeks, allowances were increased, more candidates were eligible, and commuting expenses were provided for trainees (*285*:75).

Economic Opportunity Act of 1964

The early experiences with the Manpower Development Training Act emphasized the need for adult basic education. When the Economic Opportunity Act of 1964 (EOA) became public law, it was the *first time* the federal government allotted funds directly for literacy education.

The appropriations were distributed to states which had submitted plans that complied with guidelines set up by federal administering agencies. The money was then used within the state for various adult basic education programs.

In the act, the definition of a functional illiterate shifted from "one with ability at a fifth grade level," to "one who has completed eight grades of school or less." The basic goal of the act was to provide an adult basic education program for those eighteen years or older in the hopes that, at a high school level, an adult would be able to deal with occupational training (163:885).

The programs provided under the various sections of the act were varied in an attempt to deal with the many facets of the problem.

Title 1A of the act provided the means to establish Job Corps Training Centers. These were

> urban and rural residential centers for young men and women who are 16 to 21 years of age who are not in school, unemployed and undereducated. Centers offer a coordinated program of remedial education, skill training, constructive work experience, guidance, and recreation (285: 75).

The Adult Basic Education Program (ABE) resulted from Title IIB of the 1964 act. The main purpose of the program was to provide states with grants which would be used for the development of adult basic education programs. The main emphasis was placed on teaching, in an adult content, the basic communication as well as arithmetic skills. Once a plan was written up, the state submitted it to a regional office for approval. The designs of plans might vary considerably, and funds could be used to establish ABE classes, defray instructional costs, conduct pilot studies, or improve existing services available to ABE classes.

The money was appropriated according to a formula which utilized the number of total illiterates over eighteen in the state as one of its elements. Once the state had received its allocation, the money was then distributed to local areas in a similar manner (285: 87).

Still another approach designed to help solve the problem of social, cultural, and economic deprivation came about through the Title V provision of the Economic Opportunity Act and Title XI of the Social Security Act. In the resulting Work Experience and Training Program, present and potential recipients of public assistance were singled out. Projects were designed to help needy persons "secure and retain employment, or to attain or retain capability for self-support or personal independence" (285: 60). The manner in which the goal was sought often involved basic education, medical care, counseling, job experience, or even day care for children.

The migrant and seasonal farm workers composed another group caught up in the poverty cycle. They were most affected by the Community Action Program (CAP) which received its authority from Title IIA and Title IIIB of the Economic Opportunity Act. In the phase dealing with migrant workers, financial assistance was given to qualified public and private organizations. These concerns then aided families by providing them with educational training, opportunity centers, and counseling. Teacher training was included in order to produce the qualified teachers needed to conduct the progams (285: 88).

The Higher Education Act of 1965

Although this public law did not deal directly with literacy education, certain portions provided indirect benefits to this group of people. Title V allowed for the formation of a National Teacher Corps. The main purpose of this body was to train people to teach in educationally deprived areas (285:37).

Title I called for the formation of a National Advisory Committee. The committee was composed of twenty-two members, ten representatives from government agencies and twelve lay representatives. The main function of this body was to evaluate federal programs and make a report to the President (110:382).

The Cooperative Research Act of 1954 and others

Occasionally, programs resulted from a single law and portions of others being combined. The use made of the Cooperative Research Act of 1954 was an example of such a coalition of laws. The authority received from this act, Title VII of the National Defense Education Act, and Title IV of the Elementary and Secondary Act of 1965, provided the basis of the Cooperative Research Program. Although this program did not deal directly with illiterates, it had indirect benefits for illiterates. It supported research in five main areas, including adult and vocational education. The research could be conducted by an individual or institution and prompted many educators to further investigate areas of adult illiteracy (285:26).

Adult Basic Education Act of 1966

The Adult Basic Education Act of 1966 amended the Elementary and Secondary Education Act. It created a National Advisory Committee on Adult Basic Education. This committee was designed to review the effectiveness of federally supported adult basic education programs.

The committee made several noteworthy recommendations. It recommended that adult basic education be extended through grade twelve and more emphasis be placed on reaching persons sixteen through twenty-five-years in urban areas. An increase in appropriations was recommended in order to carry out the suggestions. Finally, the committee noted that adult basic education programs were still scattered and had very little unity or communication. It suggested the solution involve national leadership, a national resource center, and standard reporting procedures (*158:* 209).

Act of November 2, 1921

A long neglected problem was that of Indian illiteracy. The Act of November 2, 1921 allowed for literacy training with the Indian population. The On-Reservation Indian Adult Education Program provided a general education for reservation Indians. This education ranged from basic reading and writing skills to high school subjects. It was designed for Indians who lacked a basic education and attempted to help them become active in community life. Approximately 32,000 Indians in 190 different communities participated in the program (*285:*63).

Federal Prison Industries Act of 1934

This act, as amended by P. L. 88-245, allowed for the operation of the Prisoner Vocational Training Program. In the program, prisoners received a variety of instruction including elementary, high school, and college topics as well as vocational training. In many prisons half the day was spent in ABE instruction, and the remaining portion in vocational training. It was finally recognized that little could be achieved in vocational training if the individual's literacy skills were greatly lacking. Slowly, steps were being taken to remedy the situation. The full range of the educational programs are financed by Federal Prison Industries, Inc. (*285:*69).

Programs

Adult Basic Education programs were numerous during the sixties because of active groups, vital legislation, and available funds. The programs conducted at state and local levels were usually funded with federal money, and varied greatly from area to area. Included in this section are samples of programs which may have involved special groups, made use of particular facilities, or been designed to fit a special piece of legislation.

The Annual Report on Adult Basic Education Programs for 1968 revealed that 456,000 adults were involved in programs during the fiscal year of 1968. This was an increase of 17 percent over the previous year. Approximately 50 percent of the enrollees were white, 43 percent black, and the remaining were nonwhite (*218*:9-10).

The report also revealed that over 60 percent of the states provided more than the required matching funds necessary to qualify for federal aid. It was interesting that the states that experienced difficulties in raising the local funds were those states whose needs were the greatest.

The teacher-training programs produced 4,348 teachers, administrators, and counselors during a four year period. By 1968, thirty-two training institutes were operating. The Special Experimental Demonstration Projects numbered twenty-one as opposed to thirteen the previous year. The purpose of these projects was to test programs and ideas related to materials, curriculum designs, and administrative systems suitable for adult basic education (*218*:12-13).

Center for Adult Basic Educational Learning

Project CABEL was an example of a Special Experimental Demonstration Project. It was a cooperative arrangement among Alexandria, Arlington, and Fairfax County public school systems, and was under the direction of George B. Griswold. The center's services were free to any adult eighteen and over who met one of the following criteria: he had not completed grade eight, he was unable to find a job because of lack of education, or he wanted to refresh his basic skills.

Classes were conducted daily, four nights a week, and on Saturday. In addition, the center provided a practicum for George Washington University students in the field of adult education. In the course of its work, the center served several hundred students (*205*:993).

Other special experimental demonstration projects included "Project Go" in Washington, D.C.; "Project Cooperation" with the Berkley Unified School System; The Urban Adult Education Institute sponsored by the Detroit Public Schools; and An Experiment in Motivating Functional Illiterates to Learn, at the Tuskegee Institute. In addition, similar projects were conducted in New Jersey, Illinois, Massachusetts, New York, Missouri, New Mexico, and Mississippi (*218*:29-31).

The Norfolk Project

During some of the retraining programs, it became obvious that a great number of people were not able to take advantage of programs without first having developed greater competencies in the basic skills. Recognizing this drawback, the Manpower Development and Training Act was amended to include adult basic education.

Those people needing basic education could be classified in three categories: the illiterate with less than grade three education, the industrial illiterate who had more than a third grade and less than an eighth grade education, and the high school graduate who had a low level of competence. Depending on the location of the school, the difference between the level of achievement and grade completed varied as much as two or three grades.

The main purposes of the Norfolk Project were to develop competencies in human relations and occupational information, retrain a technical skill, and raise the basic skill level of the individual.

The proposed project time was one year and the work involved retraining 100 men. Support was derived from USOE and the Office of Manpower, Automation, and Training. At the end of the study, it was reported that the average gain in reading ability was three years, and that personal competencies had been improved.

One unique feature of the program was that a study hour was included in order to ensure the practice that was needed, but that might not fit into the schedule at home (72:145-146).

Libraries and literacy education

Librarians and their coworkers started viewing their responsibilities differently during the mid-sixties. In the past, they felt that the function of the library was to provide books for people. The new philosophy expressed the idea that perhaps there was a responsibility the library and librarians had toward helping the illiterate adult become acquainted with the world of books, and to help him function with them.

About 1964, the Kalamazoo Library System started an Adult Reading Center in an attempt to meet this responsibility. Within the first year, over 300 pieces of material were collected. The materials could be classified into two categories. The first set of materials included books, magazines, pamphlets, and instructional programs for the students. The materials were written on readability levels one through eight, and included such topics as family life, occupations, arithmetic, social studies, and urban and rural living. The remaining materials were designed for use by the tutors and included professional books on adult psychology and teaching reading, information on literacy programs, suggested courses of study, and documented reports from agencies and literacy foundations.

Instructors were needed to conduct the program. Volunteers from various backgrounds provided the necessary tutors. In order to train them, an instructor from Operation Alphabet conducted a class one evening a week for ten weeks. After a twenty hour course in the principles of teaching illiterate adults, they began their work and another group started training.

Recognizing the lack of suitable materials, the American Association of University Women interested members in taking on the project of writing materials for illiterate adults. In order to finance the project, $1,000 in state aid funds was used in addition to contributions from private organizations. A grant from Michigan State Library also supplemented the program.

Eventually, six other centers were opened and were equipped by funds from Title II of the Economic Opportunity Act (*183*:78-79).

A library project was also initiated in Cleveland, Ohio. Cleveland claimed 50,000 functionally illiterate adults in the mid-sixties. Under the Library Services and Construction Act, the Cleveland Public Library received $111,000 for a project which aimed at getting these people into the public libraries.

In the program, a reading specialist consulted with the librarians at the branches. Social workers used a door to door approach as well as the standard methods to publicize the libraries' efforts. Appropriate books were placed in the waiting room of the Outpatient Clinic at the Metropolitan General Hospital to acquaint people with library facilities.

At the end of the first year of the program, those involved said it was difficult to evaluate the progress. According to "regular standards" the response was poor; compared to other attempts, the response was good. Perhaps the most noteworthy comment about the program was that it was an appealing approach to those who do not wish to return to formal schooling (*144*:637-38).

More and more programs for functionally illiterate and totally illiterate adults started to appear in the public library systems. Interest and concern for the disadvantaged adult even stimulated the compilation of bibliographies by the libraries. Programs and efforts along this vein are summarized in *Library Services to the Disadvantaged: A Selected List of Readings* (*42*).

Literacy training through television

During the previous decade, there were several minor attempts at literacy education through the media of television. In 1961, a new literacy program involving television was initiated in Philadelphia. The series was developed by the Philadelphia Public School Extension Division and funds were provided by the Annenberg School of Communications, University of Pennsylvania, and the Minnesota Mining and Manufacturing Company.

The project, Operation Alphabet, was produced in conjunction with WFIL TV. The format of the program was a series of 100 half-hour lessons which were run for a period of twenty weeks. Basic reading and writing skills were introduced each day. For four days, the instructor presented new reading words and one script letter for writing skill development. On the fifth day, a review lesson was presented. A 100 lesson study book was used to reinforce the lessons presented on television. Under optimal conditions, the learner would reach the level equivalent with the third grade by the end of the program. After completion of the program, students were encouraged to enroll in adult education classes.

The results of the program were displayed in the enrollment in elementary adult education classes. After the television series ended, the Philadelphia schools reported an increase of 25 percent in the adult elementary education classes.

Operation Alphabet was later distributed by the National Association for Public School Adult Education and was sent, without charge, to smaller communities. By 1966, over 100 communities had televised the programs (*145:*261).

Operation Alphabet met with various degrees of enthusiasm. In Kansas City, the program reached 8,000 out of the 25,000 illiterates in the city. In many communities, the series reached very few illiterates. Some of the workers on campaigns felt that this was due in part to the insufficient publicity.

Operation Alphabet was the topic of study in Florida when it was used in a statewide campaign against illiteracy. After eight months of instruction, an equivalent of forty-nine hours, 132 out of the 243 subjects in the study were still at a first grade level or lower. It had been anticipated the students would have progressed to grade level three. In partial explanation, the researcher noted that most of the adults stopped watching after the twentieth lesson, thus never completing the program. Other findings indicated no increase in enrollment in literacy and elementary classes, and that the home study guide made relatively little difference in the progress of the students. It also disclosed that those individuals working in groups made more progress than individuals working alone (*371*).

Chenault reported that Operation Alphabet, when used in penal institutions, met with very little success. He indicated the causes might have been inadequate facilities and a poor choice of hours for presentation (*93:*808).

In 1959, Peerson undertook to study the literacy program in an eleven county area in Alabama. Funded by the National Defense Education Act, the program consisted of telecasting the Laubach series. Volunteer teachers were placed in viewing centers and where reception was poor, the classes had direct teaching.

The results indicated that at the end of the program adult students read less well than the second graders in the Alabama schools. It was also noted that those students experiencing the direct teaching made slightly greater gains than those in viewing centers (*46*).

Other communities that experimented with commercial television were the LARK Foundation in Seattle, Washington, and the public school systems in Baltimore, Maryland, and St. Louis, Missouri (*145:*261).

The results of these studies seemed to indicate that, although lessons were presented in the privacy of a home, there was a problem in motivating the learner to take advantage of such an opportunity. The cause may have been disinterest, poor timing, or poor pacing of the program, but the conclusion seems to be that the mass approach is lacking in its ability to reach, hold, and teach the illiterate adult.

Migrant worker programs

The migrant workers of our country form a portion of society that finds it exceedingly difficult to move up the economic ladder. For the most part, these people are from rural areas and must follow the labor market. If they find themselves in an area of labor surplus or are unemployed at the end of the season's work, they must often migrate to urban areas in search of other unskilled positions.

Brice indicated the majority of migrants were from the Southern Appalachian Region, the South, selected regions of the Northwest, and Puerto Rico. These migrants are often hindered by lack of education or inability to speak the language. The fact that they are migrant, as well as being undereducated or unskilled, complicates the problem even more. Often these people, so in need of education, are unable to obtain regular help. Since they move so often, they may not be able to qualify for the educational opportunities available. The results are that the children grow into illiteracy and elders have little hope for improving their lot. Thus, the outlook is grey so long as they remain educationally lacking. With machines to perform duties in a fraction of the time, the position of the migrant worker grows increasingly perilous every day (*244:8*).

One of the many programs under contract with the USOE was a multistate project coordinated by the Southwestern Cooperative Educational Laboratory (SWCEL). Its purpose was to teach English to Spanish speaking migrant workers.

The project involved the cooperation of the University of Colorado, California State Department of Education, and the University of Arizona. Each group was responsible for a certain portion of the program. At the University of Arizona, the prime activity was to develop materials which would be appealing to this particular ethnic group. In California, the task was to determine the future direction in migrant education. Finally, at the University of Colorado, the effort was directed toward research and development of a plan to use literacy materials in remote areas.

The basic instructional package developed included thirty half-hour television programs as well as testing materials, workbooks, and teacher manuals (181:73-74).

Many of the programs conducted for migrant workers were designed to include more than just literacy training. Some efforts were designed to include all members of the family. In this way, the children would be saved from illiteracy and the adults would benefit in a similar manner.

A program conducted in Merced County, California, used this approach. Special schools were formed for migrant farm workers and their families. Each school had four separate parts: 1) a child care center for infants whose mothers wanted to attend classes; 2) a preschool for toddlers (to stimulate children from nonverbal homes); 3) curriculum for students in grades one through eight; and 4) literacy classes for adults. Thus, in one program, an attempt was made to fight illiteracy at all its stages of development (*345*).

The Home Education Livelihood Program (HELP) in New Mexico attempted to work in a similar manner with Spanish-American and Mexican-American agricultural workers. Adult and family education were available, as well as child care and remedial instruction. The center stressed basic education and vital home economic and manual skills (*317*).

Since one of the problems a migrant worker faces is his basic lack of employable skills, the Immokalee Migrant Adult Education Project in Florida approached the problem from this direction. An adult education curriculum was designed including such related subject areas as consumer education, safety, health, and science. In addition, students were provided with vocational training including testing, guidance, and counseling (*329*).

A report from Tuskegee Institute disclosed some interesting results concerning their program conducted for seasonally employed agricultural workers. The program attempted to provide prevocational and basic education for functional illiterates in seven Alabama counties. Out of 1,122 participants, all but 79 showed progress. Perhaps the general attitudes revealed were even more important. Agency referrals to the program were far less than hoped for and there was a general lack of cooperation from local administrators and others in authority. The report went on to say that both students and teachers were harassed (*337*).

This program and others like it may permit migrant workers to share in the prosperity of our country, but the programs also revealed that the problem is complex. Educating migrant workers is only one phase; changing the attitudes of those more fortunate may be a task equally as difficult.

Indians and illiteracy

The American Indians have long represented a neglected phase in the illiteracy problem. During the sixties, approximately 300,000 Indians were on reservations and looked to the Bureau of Indian Affairs for leadership in special areas such as education. The Bureau operated school systems in areas where public schools were not available, or where special programs were needed to overcome deficits in educational or social backgrounds.

On the whole, the education of Indian residents on reservations was not as adequate as that received by the rest of the population. When an Indian received a good education, there were few opportunities available and he left the reservation. The 263 schools operated by the Bureau of Indian Affairs have enrolled over 50,000 Indian children who were educationally or socially disadvantaged.

In an effort to maintain their own culture and self-respect, the Indians encouraged the use of tribal customs and their native tongues. Thus, thousands of Indian children were required to learn English as a second language. To achieve this goal, materials centers were stocked with visual and auditory materials to provide instruction and reinforcement in teaching English as a second language (*192*:38-39).

The problem of the adult Indian is as acute as that of the children. The job of educating the adult Indian for a productive life often involves extensive retraining or initial instruction. Little legislation aids the programs needed for the job.

Inmate illiteracy

At the Elmira Conference on Correction, Cortright reported that as early as 1870, the need for education within the correctional system was recognized. However, it was not until the next century that any attempt was made to deal with the problem.

As one might expect, lack of education is commonplace among most prisoners. It is estimated that approximately 98 percent of those in prison have less than a high school education. Maryland State Penitentiary reported that 70 percent of its inmates were functionally illiterate. Another interesting fact concerning inmates and lack of education was called to attention by the Director of the Wisconsin State Prison. He felt the low rate of sophisticated crimes was due to lack of education. The statistics for his prison included a high number of murderers, but only one embezzler (99:163-167).

During the sixties, many states were involved in educating prisoners. The New York State Department of Correction conducted programs in fourteen prisons. Educational programs were also conducted in Ohio, New Jersey, Florida, Alabama, and Connecticut. Many of the programs were probably similar to the one conducted in the Hartford State Jail where the program was divided into four parts. Prisoners were able to receive counseling, basic education instruction, and vocational training. Incorporated into the program was time for recreation and leisure (330).

It is now recognized that, if society is really going to rehabilitate prisoners through its correctional institutions, there is an obligation to provide the offender with education. Only in this way can there be any hope for really achieving this goal.

Project 100,000: A Department of Defense contribution

In August 1966, Secretary of Defense Robert McNamara announced the initiation of Project 100,000. The aim of the program was to assist in upgrading the educational level of the disadvantaged. The first step was taken in October 1966 when the entrance requirements for the armed forces were lowered. During the first year of the program 40,000 disadvantaged persons were accepted and 100,000 a year thereafter. By March 1969, approximately 190,000 disadvantaged individuals had entered the service. Ninety-three percent entered by means of the lowered educational standards. Even with the lowered standards, 10.5 percent of them were being rejected because they failed to pass the written test.

In studying the inductees and their progress, these facts were disclosed. The experimental group included 40 percent blacks and 47 percent from the South. In the control group, 9 percent were black and 28 percent from the South. The average percentile score for the experimental group was fourteen as opposed to fifty-four for the control group.

The project group, after exposure to the methods devised to assist them, compared favorably with the control group in basic training, skill training, promotions, and in becoming satisfactory service personnel.

Various techniques were utilized in an effort to bring these men up in their program. Tutoring and counseling were used as well as recycling. Recycling placed a man in a unit at an earlier stage of training if he needed it. Special Training Companies were organized where the trainee remained for one to thirty days depending on individual needs. In some instances, when inductees suffered from severe disadvantages, they were sent to Army Preparatory Training before they entered basic training. This preparatory training lasted six hours a day for three to six weeks. There the trainee received instruction in reading, arithmetic, citizenship, and introduction to military training.

In addition to the above program, a General Educational Development Program was conducted. It enabled inductees to receive eighth grade or high school diplomas. However, this program was conducted on off duty time and was not part of the basic project.

The cost of the project was approximately $19 million a year, an amount which averaged out to about $200 per man. The plan provided that when the armed forces were reduced, the number of individuals in the project would also be reduced (124:570).

Although they have been deeply involved with literacy programs for years, armed forces authorities still feel that literacy training is a civilian job.

Professional Activities

Teacher training

Whenever an intense and critical appraisal is made of a fast growing field, such as adult literacy education, it is quite common to discover a need for qualified specialists. When dealing specifically with adult basic education, it is not unusual to discover that existing teachers and specialists are often people who "happened" into the situation.

Yet, the sign of an emerging field is the production of qualified personnel to fill these special positions. As early as 1957, Baylor University in Waco, Texas, attacked this particular problem. Here a program designed to train literacy specialists was opened to all students. Preference was given to foreign students who would return to native homelands to train others.

In addition to the standard course work, the program provided for workshop participation and practical experience in preparing literacy publications. These courses were suitable to fulfill the requirements for a major or minor, and were also available through the correspondence division of the university (97:207-208).

The National Teacher Training Adult Basic Education Program was another attempt to provide literacy leaders. Funded through the Adult Education Act of 1966, this program was an example of a different approach to the problem.

After the appointment of a national council, a curriculum for a teacher training program was prepared. This curriculum was then used as the guide in teacher training institutes.

During the summer of 1966, the first session started with nine regional institutes being conducted. By 1967, the institutes totaled nineteen and offered a three week teacher training program and a two week administrative program (127:64-65). In 1968, twenty-seven of these institutes were being conducted in twenty-four different states. As with the previous institutes, the selected participants were paid full stipend, tuition, and travel expenses (135:96).

The objectives for these summer institutes were all quite similar. A number of participants were selected to develop skills in preparing curriculum, individualizing instruction, and developing leadership in adult basic education. The selectees recorded observations and case studies, participated in demonstrations, and practiced in learning centers. Then, they returned to their communities to share these ideas and techniques (47).

The 1970 Adult Basic Education summer institutes numbered only twenty. This may have indicated that the need for qualified specialists was not as acute as it once was. Another distinct possibility is that there was a decline in federal financial support of such programs.

In 1965, in addition to the federally supported institutes, there were workshops supported by the Ford Foundation. These workshops also helped train adult basic education teachers. The curriculum of the Inter-University Workshop on Adult Basic Education was very similar to that offered at Baylor University. It was the hope of the administrators that, once trained, the teachers would return to their states and train others (187:27).

Similar workshops and courses have been conducted by state agencies, at universities, and through special federal grants. Many believe that teacher training is still one of the primary areas of concern in literacy education today (110:349).

Research in literacy education

It soon becomes apparent that, for a developing field to mature and make positive progress, research is necessary. Until the late sixties, research in literacy education was relatively nonexistent. The few early studies dealt mainly with reading materials and methods. In 1964, an interdisciplinary conference was held at the Center for Applied Linguistics in Washington, D. C. for the Agency for International Development. At the conference, the topic of research was discussed. Participants concluded there was a definite need for research concerning the organization and administration of literacy programs (182:287).

In addition to these areas, Spaulding reported the need for literacy studies dealing with attitudes, long term effects on the economy, and longitudinal rather than point-in-time studies (182:286).

One of the more noteworthy studies done to date was conducted by Greenleigh Associates. The main objective was to evaluate four education systems using economically dependent adults. The study utilized 3,000 adults in three states and ran for a period of one year, but classes were conducted for only seventeen weeks.

Although there were results reported for each of the eight criterions, it is sufficient to note the major outcome of the study. At the end of the study, gains were revealed with all four systems. All systems raised some students to the desired eighth grade level. However, *no single system* proved significantly superior to another (24).

A second research study of general, yet significant, interest took place in Cook County, Illinois. The statistics revealed that in 1962 there were 270,000 people on relief in the county. Relief Director Raymond Hilliard indicated that the problem of unemployment and growing numbers on relief prompted the study whose purpose was to determine the extent of illiteracy among the ablebodied people on relief, and to design an educational program to help alleviate the problem.

Dr. Denton J. Brooks conducted the study in the Woodlawn area of Chicago. The resulting figures indicated that only 6.6 percent of the group had not gone as far as sixth grade. When the testing was completed, the figures revealed that 50.7 percent of the group were functioning at fifth grade level and below. The remaining percent were achieving at a level barely above fifth grade. These findings certainly emphasized the fact that there is a difference between grade completion and level of achievement, and supports the critical reading and interpretation of literacy statistics (130:1034).

In an attempt to partially solve the problem, the Board of

Education and the Welfare Administration collaborated on a citywide education program. Hilliard described the announcement in the following manner. "We added bluntly that people receiving assistance would be required to participate, reporting to the place assigned to do the work assigned, or forfeit their relief grants" (*130*:1035).

With 270,000 people on relief in the county, the anticipated turnout was 50,000 to 60,000. However, only 7,000 adults joined the program! The Cook County experience had disclosed another alarming fact — even if one has sufficient materials and instructors, the undereducated may not want to learn. If this is so, no legislation, program, nor campaign will change the situation; and the possibility of helping these people is extremely slim. With a prevailing negative attitude, they will never break the poverty chain.

Another research project conducted by Mitzel, and probably the only one of its type to date, resulted in a reading word list for adults. Based on the concept that an adult's needs in reading were concrete and immediate, the sources for these words included newspaper ads, signs in stores, the yellow pages, application blanks, menus, and TV commercials.

Words in the list were grouped according to frequency of use and not according to word difficulty. Later 5,000 words were selected from the list and compared with 5,000 words from the *Teacher's Wordbook of 30,000 Words*. The results revealed that 33 percent of the adult words were not included in the Thorndike-Lorge list. It would appear that an adult word list has the potential of being a useful tool for literacy teachers and those interested in the production of literacy materials (*159*:67).

Literacy research is increasing and rapidly becoming more sophisticated. While it is true that the number of literacy studies was greater in the sixties than ever before, the topics still awaiting investigation are limitless. With these studies may come the answer of how to help these disadvantaged adults.

Curriculum

With an expanded definition of illiteracy, it was not surprising to find educational leaders of the sixties advocating a change in curriculum to accommodate the needs of the illiterate and near-illiterate.

Literacy classes which provided the rudiments of reading and writing became obsolete and were soon replaced by classes emphasizing adult basic education. The curriculum provided the basic skills of reading, writing, and arithmetic as well as for background in such areas as family life, health, and community living.

During the mid-sixties, the United States Office of Education created a *Curriculum Guide to Adult Basic Education* which followed these new ideas *(242)*. This document was not designed to be a national curriculum but merely a guide for those who might find it helpful.

Since a curriculum must meet the basic needs of a specific group, it would be impossible to list the various endeavors made in this area. Suffice it to say that curriculums are being developed throughout the country in workshops and adult basic education institutes, by local communities and state agencies. They all revolve around the idea that the needs are immediate and the skills provided should help adults lead full lives in today's society.

Methods and Materials

Perhaps one of the more noteworthy contributions of the sixties to the field of adult literacy education was the extensive production of materials. These publications ranged from instructional materials to achievement tests and curriculum guides. For the first time in the history of literacy education, lack of suitable teaching materials was not a major problem.

So numerous were the efforts to produce appropriate level reading materials, that it is impossible to list them here. Instead, a discussion of the types of materials produced might prove more useful. Seven basic classifications are used in discussion of these materials *(48*:64-65).

The Basal Series Approach. Although none of the adult series produced are as sophisticated as those for children, the formats are similar. A series consists of several related books with one or more at each level. The vocabulary is controlled, the skills are introduced sequentially, and a workbook often accompanies the test. *Systems for Success* by Follet is an example of this type of material.

The Multilevel Package Kit. This approach was originally designed for use with children, but the concept has been expanded to adult instructional materials. The system individualizes the program by using color coded reading levels. Skills are developed at each level as the student progresses from one color to another. *The Reading Attainment System* by Grolier Educational Corporation is one such package kit.

The Experience Approach. The teacher and students are responsible for producing the actual reading materials. As a topic is discussed by the students, the teacher records the important items on the board in sentence form. The discussion is then **duplicated** and distributed to the students for reading exercises.

Programed Workbook Approach. Skills and **vocabulary** are developed through the use of frames, and the student **progresses** through the program at his own pace. Depending on the depth of the program, one or several books may be used. McGraw-Hill has published a programed workbook entitled *Programed Reading for Adults.*

Mass Media Approach. Although it is not a material, this approach is a manner in which adults have been taught to read. Based on group presentation, it utilizes film or television to present **vocabulary and develop reading skills.** *Operation Alphabet,* as utilized in many communities in the country, is one of the most typical examples of this approach.

Machine Dominated Approach. The reading program, vocabulary, and skills are presented visually by the machine and supplemented by auditory directions and instructions. Pacing of the students is fairly flexible. An example of this type of program is *Learning 100* by Educational Developmental Laboratories.

The Workbook Approach. This was one of the earliest types of material used with illiterate adults and it is still in use. The books may be several related books. Usually, stories are presented and written exercises follow the selection. Steck-Vaughn has produced a number of these books for adults.

Bibliographies

Since materials were so varied and abundant during the decade, it was logical that extensive bibliographies began to appear. These were lists of instructional books, professional literature, testing instruments, and audiovisual equipment, and were specifically designed to aid the literacy educator. The samples listed here are representative of these aids:

Bibliography for Migrant Education Programs. Washington, D. C.: Educational Systems, 1968.

Materials for Adult Basic Education: An Annotated Bibliography. Bloomington, Indiana: Indiana University, 1967.

Guide to Curriculum Materials and Testing Instruments. Washington, D. C.: Educational Projects, 1967.

Adult Basic Reading Instruction in the United States. Newark, Delaware: International Reading Association, 1967.

Bibliography of Materials for the Adult Basic Education Student. Silver Spring, Maryland: National University Extension Association, 1968.

Testing instruments

What little testing was done prior to the sixties utilized those instruments designed for children. For the first time, measuring devices designed specifically for adults were appearing on the market. With tests such as those listed below, more accurate appraisals could be made of the adult student (*48*:59-60).

Tests of Adult Basic Education. Monterey, California: California Test Bureau, 1967. This test examines the areas of reading, arithmetic, and language. It has a range from grade one through high school.

Adult Basic Learning Examination. New York: Harcourt Brace Jovanovich, 1967. This exam tests vocabulary, reading, spelling, math computation, and problem solving. The test has three levels: level one covers grades one through four; level two, grades five through eight; and level three, grades nine through twelve.

Basic Reading Inventory. Chicago: Scholastic Testing Service, 1966. This reading inventory tests the lower adult reading levels, two through four.

Individual Reading Placement Inventory. Chicago: Follett, 1968. This instrument places the student on a readability level of one through six.

Adult Basic Education Student Survey. Chicago: Follett, 1967. The survey gives an appraisal of a student's ability in reading and arithmetic.

Professional publications

The final consideration in this section on materials is that of the professional publication. The needs and questions of literacy educators prompted the publication of these books which dealt with such topics as techniques, training literacy teachers, curriculum, and background readings. The aim was to help the literacy teacher to expand and develop his knowledge of the field. Although the list is still growing, the books listed provide a sampling of these publications:

U. S. Department of Health, Education, and Welfare. Office of Education. *Curriculum Guide to Adult Basic Education: Beginning Level.* Washington, D. C.: Government Printing Office, 1966.

U. S. Department of Health, Education, and Welfare. Office of Education. *Curriculum Guide to Adult Basic Education: Intermediate Level.* Washington, D. C.: Government Printing Office, 1966.

Adult Basic Education: A Guide for Teacher Trainers.

Washington, D.C.: NAPSAE, 1966.

Brice, Edward, Roy Minnis, and Ellen Henderson. *Teaching Adults the Literacy Skills*. Washington, D. C.: General Federation of Women's Clubs.

Lanning, Frank, and Wesley Many. *Basic Education for the Disadvantaged Adult*. Boston: Houghton Mifflin, 1966.

With the production of new instructional and professional materials, testing instruments, and teacher training institutes, a decade of fairly significant progress ended. And even as it did so, the real spirit of the sixties appeared to be dwindling. Programs were being discontinued and funds were short. What is the picture for the seventies? Will the progress of the previous decade be lost in disinterest and apathy? What can and should be done in the seventies for these disadvantaged people? One can only speculate and hope we will not travel the circle we have in the past.

Summary

The election of John F. Kennedy in 1960 ushered in a decade of self-evaluation. With a critical eye, the nation began to view its international position and its national social problems.

In an attempt to cement good international relations, the Peace Corps and several other programs were established to provide for underdeveloped countries. It was during this time that the United States initially became involved in the Far East in an effort to stop the spread of Communism.

The domestic problems faced by the United States during the sixties were overwhelming. The black revolution was expanding rapidly, and often in a violent manner. As the blacks became more impatient, so did the white opposition. Large poverty pockets were discovered, and they seemed to grow as unemployment threatened more people. Many were concerned that the United States was falling behind as a leader in scientific development.

The situation was not without some hope. An active Congress during the mid-sixties produced such key legislation as the Civil Rights Act of 1964 and the Economic Opportunity Act. They also passed bills providing for tax reduction, medical care for the aged, and rent subsidy. Several major advances took place in adult literacy education during the same time. Probably more was accomplished during this decade than in all the preceding fifty years.

It was during this period that *functional illiteracy* was recognized as a problem of prominent concern. Although the percentage of absolute illiterates dropped to a new low, the number of functionally illiterate adults increased at an amazing rate. The increase in the number of functional illiterates was probably the result of redefining the term. It was no longer reasonable to consider a fifth grade education adequate for full participation in today's society. When the standard was raised, it was natural that the number of functional illiterates would increase.

For years, local and state programs had attempted to deal with the illiteracy problem with very little significant success. Lack of funds, sporadic attempts, and inadequate teachers and materials hindered progress. Events of the sixties, however, changed the picture. For the first time active participation of the federal government yielded legislation backed with financial support. It was now possible to carry out extensive programs, train teachers, and prepare materials.

Soon there was a lucrative market for adult literacy materials. Materials of the early sixties were enthusiastically received, but they lacked the quality and sophistication of the materials produced later in the decade. By the end of the sixties, instructional materials were so numerous that extensive bibliographies were compiled and distributed to literacy educators.

Along with the new materials came a new idea in literacy education. The curriculum shifted from reading, writing, and arithmetic to a more diverse one. The adult basic education class replaced the standard literacy class. A new curriculum was designed to provide the student with the basic literacy skills along with those skills needed to function in a modern society.

Attempts were made to train the needed literacy specialists. In addition to programs offered at universities, there were teacher training institutes supported by federal grants and private foundations. Professional books began to appear as did special testing instruments designed to aid the literacy teacher.

Finally, an interest in literacy research began to emerge and new avenues of the illiteracy problems were investigated. It appears that the sixties may have been a significant step toward the first sustained and continuous effort in literacy education. Only the next decade will confirm this or declare the period as just another sporadic attempt to be recorded in an already patchwork history.

Chapter Eight

1970 - : A Time of Turmoil and Uncertainty

Social Climate

A shaky beginning

The seventies ushered in a period of turmoil and upheaval in many aspects of American life. The Nixon administration managed to bring the long Vietnam struggle to a laborious close, if not a glorious victory. But the resulting antigovernmental attitudes represented only the beginning of the wave of distrust which was to follow.

The impact of Watergate and its related investigations was far reaching. It brought with it the first resignation of a United States President as well as resignations and removal of lesser officials. Equally important, it confirmed the doubts held by the general public and reaffirmed their loss of confidence in the government. This led to extensive investigations of governmental agencies.

Economic instability, a monetary crisis, and high unemployment greeted Gerald Ford as he assumed the office of President. The continuing racial revolution had expanded to include Mexican-Americans and Puerto Ricans and the problem of desegregating schools was still meeting with violence.

The growing numbers of unemployed created a strain on many of the social and economic services provided for these groups. Reductions in benefits and increases in taxes resulted in an effort to deal with the problem. The situation emphasized the fact that, although an individual could read and write, a functional level of literacy was needed to hold jobs that had more security in time of economic crisis. Without these basic skills, employment was doubtful even in the best of times.

The Statistics

A problem still exists

Statistics indicate that the rate of illiteracy which prevailed in 1900 had dropped to a new low by the end of the sixties. A population survey conducted by the census bureau in November 1969 revealed 1 percent of the population fourteen years of age and over was illiterate. In this instance, persons unable to "read and write a simple message either in English or any other language were classified as illiterate" (*232:*5). This estimate becomes the official figure for the seventies since the 1970 census contained no question concerning literacy. Therefore, the count of illiterates was approximately 1.4 million persons.

During the period from 1959 to 1969 there was a decrease of approximately 1 percent in the illiteracy rate. To account for such a decrease one needs only to observe some of the changes taking place. First, there are fewer immigrants entering the country than in years past. More schools are available and compulsory school laws insure that students attend and receive an education. Finally, the mortality of the less educated has begun to affect the literacy numbers. Each generation is replaced by a younger generation with increased schooling.

Although the statistics indicate the number of complete illiterates dropped considerably since 1900, the number of functional illiterates during the same period of time revealed a serious problem still existed. In its 1969 population survey, the census bureau related illiteracy to educational attainment. For the purpose of the survey, "it was assumed that everyone who had completed six or more years of school was literate" (*232:*1).

Samples of state forms, applications for drivers ' licenses, bank loans, and medical aid show that the average reading level of such materials is tenth grade or higher. Income tax forms have a readability level of twelfth grade or better (*314:*72). It becomes clear, then, that a person who can function at a fifth or sixth grade level is severely handicapped in today's fast moving and technological world. A ninth grade education would come closer to meeting the functional reading needs of a person living in the seventies. There are approximately 39 million people aged fourteen or older in the United States who do not have a ninth grade education. This figure drops to roughly 31 million when the base age is raised to twenty-five (*221*). These people comprise the major portion of functional illiterates.

There are many who will remain functionally illiterate simply because they fail to go to school or because they have lost interest in keeping up their skills. There is also a small portion of individuals who are unable to perform these skills because of mental disability. In spite of these exceptions, there remain many adults who are unable to functionally read and write merely because they lack the opportunity. The sum result of this situation is millions of adults who are unable to function profitably in today's society.

Legislation

The sixties revealed that active groups of people were aware of the literacy problem and its social and economic implications. This concern concretely expressed itself in the many forms of legislation and literacy projects of the sixties. There is evidence that the seventies can contribute as much to advance literacy education. The early recommendations of the National Advisory Committee on Adult Basic Education set the tone for many literacy activities taking place in the seventies.

Adult Education Act of 1969

The Adult Education Act of 1969 amended the Adult Basic Education Act of 1966. The original act provided adults with less than an eighth grade education with opportunities to improve their literacy skills. The act defined an adult as a person over sixteen and, with this limit, it had the potential of affecting millions. The amendment extended the opportunities to those with less than a twelfth grade education. With this provision, the number of adults potentially affected rose from 24 million to 69 million. Equally important, this amendment provided the funds for adult basic education programs and related teacher training, research, and demonstration projects. Many of the sample programs cited in this chapter are the direct results of this legislation (*314*:70).

Education Amendments of 1974

In August 1974, Congress passed an act which further extended and amended the Elementary and Secondary Act of 1965. This legislation, cited as the Education Amendments of 1974, can be considered one of the most important pieces of legislation in the history of literacy education to date. With its passage, reading skill received statutory recognition.

Title VII of the act outlines a National Reading Improvement Program which will continue and expand the National Right to Read Effort. The Right to Read Office will assume the responsibility of administering certain sections of this law.

The program aims to strengthen reading instruction for all groups of people and has funded sections of the bill in order to meet these goals. Reading improvement projects which aim at innovative reading programs are eligible for funding as well as programs which attempt to strengthen and expand state programs already in existence. The bill also provides grant money for special emphasis projects which utilize reading specialists in the teaching of first and second graders. Inservice reading training by special television programs is also available.

Of primary interest here is Section 723 of the act. It provides for the establishment of reading academies by institutions of higher learning or nonprofit organizations. These academies will furnish reading instruction to youths and adults who would not otherwise be able to receive instruction (*215:* 105-113).

Programs

A perspective

The format of a literacy program is determined extensively by the needs of the group it serves. During World War I, programs emphasized the complete Americanization of the foreign element. The thirties brought a depression and extensive unemployment. It was during this decade that the work relief program became popular and literacy education fit within its framework. The sixties emerged as a period of social reform. As the black and poverty revolutions of the era progressed, literacy education emerged as one of the basic rights which had been denied to these groups.

Because literacy programs of the past were usually designed for one specific group of people, they followed a singular model. Present programs provide for a much more varied selection of people and, therefore, demand a number of different models. Each group has its unique characteristics and requires special accommodating features within a program.

During the present decade candidates for adult basic education may include such groups as school dropouts, functionally illiterate high school graduates, immigrant groups, migrant workers, and youth and adult offenders in correctional institutions. Some of these groups may be decreasing in size but may have children growing into illiteracy.

Therefore, one can probably expect to see a shift from some of the more traditional patterns of literacy education. The night school program may be more effectively replaced by a daytime program with flexible time modules. Vocational training may be an essential part of certain programs while others may be designed to be remedial in nature in an effort to help those on the verge of becoming functional illiterates. In some instances, day care centers allow the attack on illiteracy to take place at two levels: the remedial level and preventative level.

The recent literature abounds with hundreds of descriptions, summaries, and final reports of literacy projects. Obviously they are too numerous to list and describe, and the author has chosen to consider some of the *types* of projects undertaken.

The National Right to Read Effort

Illiteracy as a national problem was once again brought to general public attention when the late Commissioner of Education, Dr. James E. Allen, Jr., helped launch a nationwide ten-year attack on illiteracy. In his speech, he announced that "no one shall be leaving our schools without the skill and desire necessary to read to the full limits of his capability" (383:3). A national committee was established to oversee this Right to Read Effort.

It is the aim of the program that, by 1980, 99 percent of school age children under sixteen and 90 percent over sixteen will have the use of literacy skills.

The program attacked the problem in three ways. First, it established demonstration programs. Each area involved in a demonstration project identified its special needs and planned a program around these needs. Emphasis was placed on diagnostic-prescriptive methods along with individualized instruction. Although the funding has ended for many of the projects, the aim is to extract features of these programs that can be used in local programs.

Demonstration projects included school and community based efforts. The latter directed its attention to increasing functional literacy for adult populations. A third type of demonstration project was the teacher preparation programs which were designed to prepare teachers to be qualified to teach reading in all subject areas.

The most recent development in demonstration projects is the adult reading academy. It relies, to a great extent, on private support from nonprofit organizations and its major function is to provide assistance and instruction for out-of-school adults.

The second component of the Right to Read Effort is the establishment of Right to Read States. States are eligible for funding when they give reading a high priority and are involved in basic activities to implement these statewide approaches. A state must be involved in evaluating the needs of the state, developing activities to meet these needs, preparing reading directors, and maintaining reading programs.

The third and final component of the Right To Read Effort is the national impact programs. These programs have been designed to reach massive numbers of people. Many of the activities fall into the classification of materials dissemination. Reports by the International Reading Association, tutor training packages and filmstrips, and the validation of packaged programs represent some of the activities being conducted. In addition, promotional and informational activities come under this phase. Surveys, television spots, and promotional films represent some of the efforts in this area (*378*).

The National Right to Read Effort has received financial support from such laws as the Adult Education Act of 1966 and the Educational Amendments of 1974.

Appalachian Adult Basic Education Demonstration Center

An example of a demonstration center is the Appalachian Adult Basic Education Demonstration Center located at Morehead State University in Kentucky. The agency served forty-five counties in a total of thirteen states, including Alabama, Georgia, Mississippi, Kentucky, New York, Maryland, North Carolina, Ohio, Pennsylvania, South Carolina, Tennessee, Virginia, and West Virginia. Each state module was involved in at least one type of project. Projects varied greatly in nature and dealt with areas such as teacher training, demonstrations, research or agents for change (*304*).

In some instances, the results of these efforts yielded definite answers to literacy education questions, but others merely gave direction for further study. Both the Ohio module (*303*) and the New York module (*304*) studied home instruction in some form. In both cases, the modules reported better results with home instruction than with traditional classroom instruction.

A separate study conducted in Montana also investigated home instruction for adults. Project Homebound (*338*) was a three phrase project utilizing volunteers in the home. The final report concluded that the home approach was an effective vehicle in literacy instruction. These investigations suggest, however, that there are many variables affecting home instruction.

Several units directed attention toward evaluation or development of materials. In Gadsden, Alabama, videotape recordings were utilized to supplement the curriculum designed for adult basic education. A note of caution was inserted, however. It was felt the demand made of ABE specialists ought to be limited because these people lack training in such highly technical areas. The Ohio module, using teacher-made supplementary materials, came to a similar conclusion. Mississippi, in addition to its mobile learning center, published a low-readability level newspaper called the *Appalachian News*. The paper was well received by ABE teachers (*304*).

Some centers investigated motivation and behavior. The unit in Maryland found the typewriter to be influential in keeping adults in class. In West Virginia, positive changes were evident in the behavior of ABE students' children.

At Morehead State University, a center was established to evaluate materials and to provide training for professionals and paraprofessionals. A graduate program was established and ABE Teacher Training Workshops were conducted.

Library efforts

In recent times, there have been cooperative efforts between libraries and adult basic education programs (*292*). One common way for a library to maintain a relationship with adult basic education programs is through the bookmobile. The Southern Appalachian Public Library and the Columbus County Public Library in North Carolina maintained mobile units. On occasion, libraries having the resources or grants choose to actually conduct classes for illiterates. The Chattanooga Public Library is such an example. When the classes were discontinued, emphasis was placed on working with preschool children in order to prevent illiteracy. In Floyd County, Kentucky, emphasis was placed on contacting illiterates and making nonprinted materials more available (*321*).

Materials bibliographies were often compiled for adult basic education use. The Library Materials Research Project was a related activity conducted at the University of Wisconsin. The purpose of the project was to establish criteria for the evaluation of library materials. In this instance, the materials were those being used to bridge the literacy skills (*292*).

The cooperative efforts between libraries and adult basic education programs are highly volatile. In many instances, the continuation of such cooperative efforts is subject to the availability of funds; with the termination of funds comes the termination of programs.

The military and illiteracy

Times of national conflict have revealed that the military is involved in literacy education by necessity, if not by choice. Now that the draft has been replaced by a volunteer army, this literacy problem is even a greater concern to the military. McGoff and

Harding (327) confirm this in their report on literacy training in the Armed Forces.

Standards set for literacy are sixth grade achievement for the Air Force and fifth grade for the Army and Navy, but these levels fall short of the more recently suggested seventh grade level (355). The average entry grade in a remedial program is 3.7 (327:23). The amount of instructional time devoted to these remedial programs varies. The Air Force spends approximately 260 hours during the course of thirteen weeks, while the Army makes use of a six week period totaling 180 hours. The Navy program varies from installation to installation with the time of instruction ranging from 100 hours to 210 hours (327:39-42).

The methods and materials used in the instructional programs varied. *Reader's Digest,* SRA Reading Laboratories, and prepared service materials were frequently used. However, in the light of needs and time, McGoff indicated a need to investigate the effectiveness of different methods and materials.

The Human Resources Research Organization, sponsored by several governmental agencies, has conducted a program of military literacy research (356) which represents the longest sustained program of literacy research by the military. There were two goals. The first was to study the literacy problem by identifying the literacy skills needed to perform the military jobs. Project REALISTIC and Project READNEED were the vehicles used to achieve this end. The results showed that reading demands of army jobs exceeded the abilities of many personnel and that a positive relationship existed between reading ability and job proficiency. Most important was the fact that even the remedial training goals fell short of reading demands.

The second goal of the research was to design a literacy program which would correct these problems. Project FLIT (Functional Literacy) was initiated as a prototype training program for the Army. The program was designed for use in a six week period. An inductee was tested and sent to basic combat training. After successful completion of that program, he entered the FLIT program level. In the initial phase of FLIT, the candidate is tested again. If the results are lower than a given score, he enters a job reading program. The program is set up in modules so that a student can be retested and recycled through portions if necessary. Results indicate the exit scores are 2.5 grades higher than the entry scores.

Methods and Materials

The materials used with adults in the past were designed

specifically for children and their interests. Educators even used the same techniques and approaches with adults as they did with children. The results were often disinterested students and little progress.

The previous decade brought an abundance of adult literacy materials—some good and some bad. The market grew, materials became more sophisticated, and now there is probably an ample number and a variety of good instructional materials for use with any type of adult group.

In fact, *variety* is one of the key words for the seventies. A successful literacy program will have a variety of teaching-learning materials in its plan. This might include adult basic readers, programed workbooks, multilevel kits, correlated worktexts, and machine-oriented programs. Audiovisual equipment has played a more significant role in programs of the seventies.

Computer assisted instruction

The newest area of investigation in literacy — computer assisted instruction — has been a controversial topic. Golub (*312*) described a CAI program designed at Pennsylvania State University. This program was a career oriented program for youths. It attempted to bring the reading levels of these youths up to an eighth grade level, to use work oriented materials to prepare them for jobs, and to provide career information. The Pennsylvania program found that self-pacing, active response of the student, and immediate feedback were the positive features of such a program. They also recorded the positive feelings of the subjects as an asset of the program. However, when comparing the progress of students using CAI with those using a programed text, they found no significant difference in the final results (*291*). The work at Pennsylvania State University has yielded a useful reference list for those interested in computer assisted instruction.

Lawrence Stolurou, director of CAI projects at the Harvard Computing Center, reported interesting results on a feedback study (*296*:30). Students received various types of feedback to their responses in a computer assisted instruction setting. Groups received a right or wrong response, right response with added encouragement, wrong response with encouragement, or encouragement on either response. The results were that students with high aggression did better with no response of evaluation. Since the characteristics of the individual make a difference, CAI may be more suited for certain students than for others.

The Raleigh Adult Learning Center at North Carolina State

University undertook a study of CAI with functionally illiterate adults. It investigated several aspects of CAI (295). Using an IBM 1500 and a more simplified system, the cost per pupil per hour was estimated. The results indicated that even with simplified systems, CAI is more expensive than conventional systems of instruction. The question arose as to whether it could bring special benefits to students.

Since ABE students will not exert effort to generate answers, the progress that can be made with CAI, even with error responses, is considered a very positive feature. The branching that is used is based on an individual's response and is more flexible than that found in programed instruction. Finally, with CAI, students were less likely to take long breaks between short instructional periods than they were with programed instruction.

Important negative aspects of CAI were also discovered. Many technical problems occurred in storage and programing, thus creating a need for a systems programer. The hardware itself intimidated learner and created anxieties. Such tensions made the individual sensitive to irrelevant stimuli. For those students with hearing or visual problems the use of CAI was more difficult since they had to observe characters and use audio in a room with high noise level.

One aspect of the investigation studied the use of programed books in conjunction with a minicomputer. The computer provided immediate feedback on a frame. This Instant Process Controller (IPC) did not make use of audio. It merely responded with a red or green light. A red response brought a proctor to the student for assistance.

The findings of the Raleigh Adult Learning Center direct attention to several avenues for future research. First, the center found CAI to be costly and intimidating to students. Second, the gains by students were not significantly higher than those achieved with other systems. The report further stated, "CAI in its conventional forms should not be explored any further at present for ABE students" (295: 53). It also recommended further investigation of IPC systems, the development of mobile IPC systems, and standardization of computer software and related hardware.

Television

Although the sixties revealed that the television approach was basically not successful, it appears that interest in literacy education via this medium will continue during the seventies. This may be due in part to the popularity of such programs as *Sesame Street* and *The Electric Company*. In any case, adult programs will have to overcome the problems of time, funding, follow up, and apathy on the part of potential students.

In 1970, the National Institute on Instructional Television and Adult Basic Education was held at the University of Maryland. The conference brought together professional educators and television producers and directors from eighteen states. During the three week institute, the participants spent time learning about one another's professional fields, writing and producing scripts, and designing plans for use when they returned to their home states. Follow-up activities, consultants, seminars, and copies of videotapes were provided for the participants. The project received USOE funding for a period of fifteen months during the early seventies (287).

More recently the Right to Read Effort has made plans for producing two types of literacy programs, one for English speaking adults and the other for Spanish speaking adults. The half-hour sessions will be available to local stations and printed material will supplement the programs (288).

Individualized instruction

The second key word for the seventies is *individualize*. Educators attempt to teach the student at his individual level, using his individual interests, and in a style that will best suit his individual needs. Therefore, a diagnostic approach will be used more often in literacy programs since it readily lends itself to an individualized program.

When using a diagnostic approach, the instructor evaluates the student's needs and prescribes activities and materials to remedy the problem. Unlike some approaches in which an evaluation is made only at the beginning and end of the program, the diagnostic approach is dominated by frequent informal retesting and prescription. The result of the approach is a singularly unique program for each student. Over twenty Individually Prescribed Instruction sites scattered over the United States have studied this approach. The results show IPI students making greater gains (297).

Some companies are involved in designing materials to fit this concept. The curriculum is in a series of packages containing concepts, objectives, multimedia, testing and in-depth problems. Nea Rad Corporation of Ft. Lauderdale and the Materials Dissemination Center in South Laguna, California, have pioneered this area.

The aids

Ideally, the teaching materials used with such approaches as IPI will be ordered for skill development, written at a low readability level, and will develop content areas and skills for periodic testing. Since no single publisher's materials can meet all the criteria, selections must be made with great care.

Handbooks such as the one by Friedman and Knight (*310*) provide a source for materials. Annotated bibliographies are readily available and deal with all aspects of literacy. Rosen (*342*) has provided an annotated bibliography on ABE tests; Thomas (*359*), one for English as a second language; and the Michigan State Department of Education (*282*), one on instructional materials. State departments of education and the ERIC indexes can provide more information as needed by the ABE specialist.

Professional Activities

Professional training

It is now a generally accepted fact that the task of literacy education needs to be conducted by competent and qualified adult basic education instructors. Many times in the past this has been stated, but very little concrete action was aimed at achieving this end.

With the aid of the Adult Education Act of 1966, yearly teacher training institutes were conducted. They aimed at preparing teachers from various geographic areas. The institutes included experiences for adult basic education leaders and teachers. By the seventies, the institutes were expanded to include counselors and administrators as well as teachers and leaders. These groups returned home to share their experiences with other adult basic education people. Emphasis was placed on four kinds of institutes: national, multiregional, regional, and special populations (*250*).

As part of its work, the Appalachian Adult Basic Education Demonstration Center conducted a Teacher Trainer Reading Workshop. Intensive training in reading skills, diagnosis, and instruction was given. The purpose of the workshop was to prepare trainer teams to enter communities and conduct reading workshops (*286*). These workshops and institutes attempted to quickly train large numbers of instructors and leaders in adult basic education. They emphasized the need for more preservice programs such as the ones at Baylor and Syracuse Universities.

Literacy research: mobility, motivation, and interest

As the field of adult basic education matures and develops, it is obvious that mere opinion will not suffice to answer the many educational questions that arise. The adult educator has the responsibility of basing his philosophy on something more substantial. Literacy research is that "something."

The sixties foreshadowed the importance of research, but it appears that the seventies may be the decade in which many of the right questions will be asked and, hopefully, answered. Many of the federally supported projects have been designed to promote research of these crucial questions. The topics are varied and range from mobility and motivation to materials and performance criteria.

Rowan and Northrup (*343*) reported on the impact of educational programs on upward mobility of disadvantaged workers. They cited several companies conducting programs designed to improve educational qualifications to move unskilled workers to progression lines or maintenance.

The results were not encouraging. The ABE programs promised much more than they were able to deliver. Very few finished the course of study and when they did, the relationship between training and promotion was not evident. Programed materials were unsuccessful (particularly with those who lacked literacy) and packaged programs did not take into consideration cultural characteristics. Motivation appears to be an underlying factor here and the findings of Rowan and Northrup would appear to give this direction for future research.

A pilot study conducted at the University of Missouri investigated the topic of interest and motivation (*320, 344*). Fifty semiliterates were used in the study. Group A was instructed in low readability but high interest material. Group B received instruction from materials chosen for their utility in daily life. Both groups made significant gains during four months of instruction although Group B had significantly greater gains than Group A. Group B had more positive feelings about their program. Thus, the findings concluded that increased performance was more closely related to motivation than materials.

Reinforcement is an important aspect in the adult learning process and Lowther (*325*) approached this topic in an unusual manner. Using the rewards of money and praise, she tried to determine the relative effectiveness of these two types of teacher rewards in reading. For each correct response, a student received five cents. The correct responses were substantially higher with money than without. Thus, the need for positive and immediate reinforcement is again emphasized.

Stein (*353*) directed her attention to the problem of ethnic differences. She developed a basic word list for adult black illiterates. The study used a sample of 263,727 words from interviews with 128 black informants. Although the list does not take into consideration the grammatical structure of black language, this list can be an important tool for the production of ethnic materials.

Whenever the subject of illiteracy is studied or discussed, the problem of definition arises. It is the very root of the problem. In past years we have not studied the kind and degrees of reading needed in an industrial society. Several studies have been conducted using a new concept of literacy.

Lou Harris and Associates were commissioned to conduct a study on functional reading ability (*300*). They sought to identify those who were not able to respond to practical tasks of everyday life. In order to evaluate this "survival literacy," a test was assembled from ads, application forms, and directions. The results showed that 4 percent of the population suffered from serious deficiencies (*300:4*).

The University of Texas has been conducting a study which attempts to describe functional literacy in behavioral terms and develop devices to assess it (*334*). This Adult Performance Level Study was initiated in 1971. The study defines literacy as "the application of a set of skills to a set of general knowledge areas which result from the cultural requirements that are imposed on numbers of culture" (*334:* 3). These skills include reading, writing, speaking, listening, problem solving, and computation as they apply to consumer economics, occupational knowledge, government health and community resources. Surveys have been conducted in these areas in order to describe literacy in behavorial terms. Both the Harris Study and Adult Performance Level Study reflect the new trend of viewing literacy as a broader concept.

Organizations and resources

In an overview of recent literacy progress, Parke (*336*) cites a number of technical breakthroughs in the field. Among these she refers to the pooling of resources. Investigations during the course of this book have revealed that, in many instances, records of attempted programs, instructional materials, or teaching guides have been lost to historical recording because there was no central body to collect and store these reports. The results of many successful programs may never have reached the confines of the town and, even then, may never have been summarized for local use.

The need for a clearinghouse facility has been recognized as an important step in unifying programs and sharing ideas on adult basic education. The Center for Urban Education in New York City, the Center for Applied Linguistics and the National Multimedia Center for Adult Basic Education in Washington conduct research and disseminate such information. The Educational Resources Information Center has a clearinghouse for literacy at Syracuse University and has been most effective and efficient in its distribution of information.

These resources will become even more useful as organizations interested in literacy add to the store of knowledge. Such organizations include the National Association for Public Continuing and Adult Education, the American Library Association, the Adult Education Association, the International Reading Association, and the National Affiliation for Literacy Advance (*301*). Involved in various aspects of literacy education and research, these organizations have the potential of fashioning the progress of literacy education in the present decade.

Summary

A great deal was learned about literacy education during the sixties. In fact, more was learned than in the total sixty years preceding that decade. The seventies now have the potential of using what has been learned and making significant progress.

Legislation is providing the financial backing needed to carry on such an extensive project. These funds are being directed toward research, teacher training, developing materials and leadership, and providing resources. No area of literacy education need be neglected during the present decade. This includes unifying existing programs. There is an effort to coordinate all the literacy activities throughout the country, an important step which is vital to the success of future literacy plans.

Publishers are providing a variety and abundance of good teaching materials. Low level materials designed to interest and teach the adult are available at reasonable prices. They cover areas which range from vocational topics to health and safety in the home. There is now something for everyone.

Finally, the educator is recognizing his professional responsibility. He is studying the resources available to him and is making better use of them. Attempts to establish a clearinghouse to share ideas on literacy education may soon yield tangible results. Also, with his background and experience, the adult educator can help train qualified personnel for literacy education.

This decade has the potential of becoming the most significant period in the history of literacy education. With strong and informed leaders, financial support, and sustained interest, adult literacy education has a chance of becoming an integral part of the educational system. Only time will tell if we are ready to enter this new era.

Epilogue

What Formula for the Future?

If, indeed, we learn from the past, this history of adult literacy education should provide direction for the future. All history is subject to interpretation and the history of literacy education is no exception. In an effort to maintain historical accuracy, however, the author has refrained from personal commentary until now.

At this point, an important question remains: Do we, as a nation, realize the seriousness and extent of illiteracy and, if so, how shall we go about dealing with this problem in the future? History tells us that we have realized the seriousness of illiteracy on many occasions in the past. In most instances, it was called to attention because of commonly shared crises. The attention given to illiteracy programs during World War I and World War II is an excellent illustration of this awareness. Currently, literacy awareness is displayed through legislation which is being proposed and passed by Congress. However, there has never been a sustained and continuous effort made in this direction. Unless there is, success will always be elusive.

Before a problem can be solved, it must be clearly identified. In literacy education one starts by defining the terms *illiterate* and *adult*. An illiterate has been described in the past by his inability to write his name, his inability to read and write a simple message in English, or by the grade level he has failed to complete. In some instances, grade achievement was the measure of literacy. More recently the concept has taken on a broader interpretation as in the Harris Study and the Adult Performance Level Study. In these instances, literacy was viewed in terms of life related tasks.

The definition must be demanding enough to allow a person to function comfortably in today's society and yet realistic enough to be achieved by most people. It must be a flexible definition which allows for change as society changes and makes different demands on its people. It may make use of grade level, life related tasks, performance on literacy tests, or any combination of these factors.

As was the case with the term *illiterate*, the term *adult* is one which has had many definitions. In the past, an adult could have been a person of age ten, fourteen, fifteen, sixteen, eighteen, twenty, or even twenty-five. A sound rationale should be developed and a basic age established for an adult. Although defining adult is much simpler than defining illiterate, the task is no less important.

In order to see what literacy progress is and is not being made, it is imperative to conduct research. The uniformity and compatability of definitions are absolute necessities for scientific studies of comparison. This is the starting point.

Once the area of definition has common agreement, the possibilities are limitless for literacy research. At an interdisciplinary conference held at the Center for Applied Linguistics in 1964, organization and administration were identified as areas in literacy education needing research and these topics still are timely. More recently, Spaulding indicated the need for longitudinal studies as opposed to point in time studies.

Many federal programs have made provisions for such research. This is a step forward, but it represents only a beginning. There is a need to develop a systematic and organized body of research which would permeate all areas of literacy education.

Once a topic has been investigated at a certain level or stage and the findings confirmed in other settings, there is a responsibility on the part of educators to base their actions upon the research. The results give direction for new research and modifications and improvements of old theories and practices. Ignoring the research findings is ignoring professional responsibility.

In the future, programs, methods, and materials need to be geared more toward the individual and his respective needs and goals. Thus, there will be many different kinds of ABE programs, depending on the populus served. Great variations might exist between the structure of an ABE program designed for an urban setting and one designed for a rural area.

Once a program is in operation, the vehicle for carrying the needed literacy skills to the individual is diagnostic-prescriptive teaching. The important prerequisite for this type of teaching is a well trained ABE teacher. This training might take the form of inservice education, summer teacher training institutes, or preservice courses. Whatever form is used, the training is essential to carry out successful diagnostic-prescriptive teaching.

In the past, literacy programs have appeared and disappeared as crises, funds, or interest fluctuated. This is not good enough for the future. If ABE programs are to be truly effective, they must become a permanent and integral part of the existing educational system. Such a relationship will provide for the continuity of programs, which is essential if significant literacy progress is to be made.

No single solution to the problem of illiteracy exists, only avenues to investigate and probe. Some of these have been mentioned: common working definitions, research, techniques, and the structure of the educational system. There is, however, still another problem which has been identified and discussed in the past and yet remains neglected. This is the area of attitude and motivation.

From time to time, reports from projects and research mention the attitudes of participants in the final summaries. These summaries often include incidental phrases and statements which reflect the lack of interest and enthusiasm the adult learner demonstrates.

The television studies have consistently reported a problem in motivating the adult to take advantage of such learning opportunities. Studies using monetary rewards for the learner have demonstrated that many adult students operate at an extrinsic motivational level. This level is the most elemental and is more easily destroyed by outside factors.

In his extensive study of Army illiterates, Goldberg addressed the problem of motivation. In most civilian situations he indicated that the illiterate does not see the benefit in learning to read and write. Consequently, there is no desire to learn.

Years after Goldberg made this observation, it was illustrated with alarming clarity in Cook County, Illinois. The Welfare Administration and the Board of Education set up an educational program designed for relief recipients who lacked literacy skills. Those receiving relief assistance were required to attend classes if they lacked reading skills. If they did not attend, they would forfeit their money. With 270,000 people on relief, only 7,000 joined the program. The undereducated did not want to learn.

Attitude, then, is the hidden variable of the literacy problem. At times it is an almost imperceptible factor and yet it is ever present. It is this factor which will determine the ultimate success or failure of literacy programs, for there is no program nor legislation that can force a person to learn if he does not *want* to learn. Attitude is the very core of the problem and the factor which is virtually impossible for educators to control.

Millions of Americans will remain functionally illiterate by choice and their children may grow up assimilating this same indifference. If the idea sounds disturbing, it should.

With these facts in mind, there are two directions which must be followed. First, opportunities for learning should not be denied to those adults who are motivated and want to move away from illiteracy. The suggestions made earlier show what avenues need to be pursued in order to provide effective programs for these people.

Next, it must be acknowledged that there is a large group of adults who will not be reached. Recognition of this fact provides the second direction. We, as a nation, must commit ourselves to preventative measures and focus our attention on elementary and secondary schools. Only when we concentrate on producing literate students can we hope to affect the statistics.

This means that all teachers, at both elementary and secondary levels, must be well trained in the area of reading. The curriculum needs to actively emphasize the literacy skills from the primary grades through high school. Finally, we must institute a minimal reading achievement level as part of graduation requirements. We must devote our time, energy, money, and expertise to this end.

There is no absolute formula for the future, but the key idea is not the elimination of illiteracy; rather it is the prevention of illiteracy.

Selected Bibliography

Books

1. *Adult Basic Education: A Guide for Teacher Trainers.* Washington, D.C.: NAPSE, 1966.
2. Aker, George, and Wayne Schroeder (Eds.). *National Institute on Resources Development and Utilization in Adult Basic Education.* Tallahassee: Florida State University, 1970.
3. American Association for Adult Education. *Handbook for Adult Education.* New York: American Association for Adult Education, 1934.
4. Anderson, Darrell, and John A. Niemi. *Adult Education and the Disadvantaged Adult.* Syracuse, New York:EricClearinghouse on Adult Education, 1969.
5. Bassett, John Spencer. *A Short History of the United States* (3rd ed.).New York: Macmillan, 1939.
6. Beals, Ralph A., and Leon Brody. *The Literature of Adult Education.* New York: American Association for Adult Education, 1941.
7. Beard, Charles A., and William C. Bagley. *The History of the American People.* New York: Macmillan, 1919.
8. Beglinger, Nina J. *Constructive Lessons in English for the Foreign Born.* Boston: Gorham Press, 1922.
9. Beglinger, Nina J. *Methods in Adult Elementary Education* (rev. ed.). New York: Charles Scribner's Sons, 1928.
10. *Bibliography for Migrant Education Programs.* Washington, D.C.: Educational Systems, 1968.
11. *Bibliography of Materials for the Adult Basic Education Student.* Silver Spring, Maryland: National University Extension Association, 1968.
12. Blum, John M., et al. *The National Experience, Part II: A History of the United States Since 1865* (2nd ed.). New York: Harcourt Brace Jovanovich, 1968.
13. Campbell, John C. *The Southern Highlander and His Homeland.* New York: Russell Sage Foundation, 1921.
14. Cartwright, Morse A. *Ten Years of Adult Education.* New York: Macmillan, 1935.
15. Cass, Angela W. "Fundamental and Literacy Education for Native and Foreign Born Adults," in Malcolm S. Knowles (Ed.), *Handbook of Adult Education in the United States.* Chicago: Adult Education Association of USA. 1960.
16. Clark, Harold F., and Harold Sloan. *Classrooms in Factories.* Rutherford, New Jersey: Institute of Research, Fairleigh Dickinson University. Distributed by New York University Press, 1958.
17. Conference on Reading. "Army Experiences with Readers and Reading and Their Implications for Postwar Education," *Appraisal of Current Practices in Reading,* 7, Supplementary Educational Monograph No. 61. Chicago: University of Chicago, 1946.
18. Current, Richard, Harry Williams, and Frank Freidel. *American History: A Survey.* New York: Alfred A. Knopf, 1961.

19. Dentler, Robert A., and Mary Ellen Warshauer. *Big City Dropouts and Illiterates.* New York: Center for Urban Education, 1965.
20. *Educational Technology.* Silver Spring, Maryland: National University Extension Association, 1968.
21. Fisher and Call. *English for Beginners.* Boston: Ginn, 1917.
22. Goldberg, Samuel. *Army Training of Illiterates in World War II.* New York: Teachers College, Columbia University, 1951.
23. Gray, William S., Wil Lou Gray, and J. W. Tilton. *The Opportunity Schools of South Carolina.* New York: American Association for Adult Education, 1932.
24. Greenleigh Associates. *Field Test and Evaluation of Selected Adult Basic Education Systems.* New York: Greenleigh Associates, 1966.
25. Gudschinsky, Sarah C. *Handbook on Literacy.* Norman, Oklahoma: University of Oklahoma, 1953.
26. *Guide to Curriculum Materials and Testing Materials.* Washington, D. C.: Educational Projects, 1967.
27. Hayes, Alfred S. (Ed.). *Recommendations of the Work Conference on Literacy.* Washington, D. C.: Center for Applied Linguistics of the Modern Language Association, 1965.
28. Hicks, John D., and George E. Mowry. *A Short History of American Democracy* (2nd ed.). Boston: Houghton Mifflin, 1956.
29. Hicks, John D., George E. Mowry, and Robert E. Burke. *The American Nation* (4th ed.). Boston: Houghton Mifflin, 1955.
30. Isenberg, Irwin (Ed.). *The Drive Against Illiteracy.* New York: H. Wilson Co., 1964.
31. Jones, Emily M., Mary D. Gray, and Wil Lou Gray. *Bible Story Readers.* Richmond, Virginia: Johnson Publishing, 1922.
32. Knight, Edgar W., and Clifton L. Hall. *Readings in American Educational History.* New York: Appleton-Century-Crofts, 1951.
33. Knox, A. B. *Adult Basic Education.* New York: Center for Adult Education, Teachers College, Columbia University, 1967.
34. Kotinsky, Ruth. *Elementary Education of Adults.* New York: American Association for Adult Education, 1941.
35. Kreks, Annette B. *Teaching Adults to Read: Research and Demonstration in a Program of Volunteer Community Action, A Report of the Project for Adult Literacy.* Boston: Massachusetts Council for Public Schools, 1969.
36. Laubach, Frank. *Streamlined English.* New York: Macmillan, 1956.
37. Laubach, Frank C., and Robert Laubach. *Toward World Literacy.* Syracuse, New York: Syracuse University Press, 1960.
38. Levine, Louis. *The Women's Garment Workers: A History of the International Ladies' Garment Workers Union.* New York: B. W. Huebsch, 1924.
39. MacCormick, Austin H. *Education of Adult Prisoners.* n.p.: National Society of Penal Information, 1931.
40. Mangano, Joseph A. (Ed.). *Strategies for Adult Basic Education,* Perspectives in Reading No. 11. Newark, Delaware: International Reading Association, 1969.
41. *Materials for Adult Basic Education: An Annotated Bibliography.* Bloomington, Indiana: Indiana University, 1967.
42. New Jersey Library Association, Human Relations Committee. *Library Service to the Disadvantaged: A Select List of Readings.* Trenton, New Jersey: Public and School Library Services Bureau, 1969.
43. Noble, Stewart G. *A History of American Education* (rev. ed.). New York: Rinehart, 1954.
44. Ogden, Jean, and Jess Ogden. *These Things We Tried.* Charlottesville, Virginia: University of Virginia, Extension Division, 1949.
45. Otto, W., and D. Ford. *Teaching Adults to Read.* Boston: Houghton Mifflin, 1967.
46. Peerson, N. *An Experiment with Evaluation in the Eradication of Adult Illiteracy by Use of Television Instruction Over a State Educational Television Network Supplemented by Supervised Group Viewing and by the Related Use of Project Supplied Materials of Instruction.* Florence, Alabama: Florence State College, 1961.
47. *Project to Train Teachers in Adult Basic Education Curriculum Development: Final Report.* Columbus: Ohio State University, Center for Adult Education, 1969.

48. Smith, Edwin. *Literacy Education for Adolescents and Adults*. San Francisco, California: Boyd and Fraser, 1970.
49. Smith, Nila Banton. *American Reading Instruction*. Newark, Delaware: International Reading Association, 1965.
50. Stewart, Cora Wilson. *Country Life Readers* (two books). Richmond, Virginia: B. F. Johnson, 1915-1916.
51. Stewart, Cora Wilson. *Moonlight Schools for the Emancipation of Adult Illiterates*. New York: E. P. Dutton, 1922.

Articles

52. "Abolition of Illiteracy," *School and Society*, 90 (April 7, 1962), 155-156.
53. "Acquiring Literacy," *School and Society*, 32 (August 23, 1930), 268.
54. "Adult Education and Radio Broadcasting," *School and Society*, 30 (November 2, 1929), 595-596.
55. "Adult Education Under the Works Progress Administration," *School and Society*, 48 (November 26, 1938), 692-694.
56. "Advisory Committee on National Illiteracy," *School and Society*, 30 (November 23, 1929), 708.
57. "Advisory Committee on National Illiteracy," *School and Society*, 30 (December 14, 1929), 807.
58. "Advisory Committee on National Literacy," *School Life*, 15 (January 1930), 91-92.
59. ALA Adult Services Division. "Books for Adults Beginning to Read," *Wilson Library Bulletin*, 40 (September 1965), 66-70.
60. Alderman, L. R. "Emergency Relief and Adult Education," *School and Society*, 38 (December 2, 1933), 717-719.
61. Anderson, C. A. "In Adult Basic Reading Programs, Are We Teaching Students or Systems?" *Adult Leadership*, 16 (November 1967), 179-181.
62. Aptheker, H. "Literacy, the Negro, and World War II," *Journal of Negro Education*, 15 (October 1946), 595-602.
63. Askov, Eunice N., and others. "Development of Specific Reading Skills in Adult Education," *Twentieth Yearbook of the National Reading Conference*, December 1970,1-15.
64. Bagley, William C. "Illiteracy and Near-Illiteracy in the Selective Service Age Groups," *School and Society*, 55 (June 6, 1942), 633-634.
65. Barnes, Robert F. "Materials, Methods, and Programs for Literacy Education," *Review of Educational Research*, 35 (June 1965), 218-223.
66. Benschoten, J. A. "Just to Read and Write!" *World's Work*, 59 (December 1930), 77-80.
67. Berg, P. C. "Illiteracy at the Crossroads," *Adult Leadership*, 9 (June 1960), 47-48.
68. "Big Lift for Illiterates," *Life*, January 28, 1957, 47.
69. Blaug, M. "Literacy and Economic Development," *School Review*, 74 (Winter 1966), 393-418.
70. Blodgett, James H. "Illiteracy in the United States," *Educational Review*, 8 (October 1894), 227-235.
71. Boardman, G. C. "Literacy Has New Meanings," *Wisconsin Journal of Education*, 89 (March 1957), 19.
72. Brazziel, William F. "Basic Education in Manpower Retraining Programs," *Adult Leadership*, 13 (November 1964), 145-146.
73. Brazziel, William F. "Revolution in Materials for the Undereducated Adults," *Audiovisual Instruction*, 11 (April 1966), 254-256.
74. Brickman, W. W. "Literacy Is Not Enough," *School and Society*, 78 (November 28, 1953), 171-172.
75. Brunner, E. deS. "Educational Status of American Adults," *Teachers College Record*, 44 (February 1943), 355-360.
76. Brunner, E. deS. "Trends in Educational Attainment 1940-1950," *Teachers College Record*, 55 (January 1954), 191-196.
77. Butterfield, K. L. "Adult Education among Rural People," *Journal of Adult Education*, 1 (October 1929), 388.
78. Caliver, Ambrose. "Adult Education of Negroes," *School Life*, 29 (October 1946), 26.

79. Caliver, Ambrose. "A Literacy Project Draws to A Close," *School Life*, 32 (February 1950), 74-75.
80. Caliver, Ambrose. "For A More Literate Nation," *School Life*, 40 (December 1957), 13-14.
81. Caliver, Ambrose. "Illiteracy and Manpower Mobilization," *School Life*, 33 (June 1951), 131-133.
82. Caliver, Ambrose. "Needed: Another Crash Program," *Adult Leadership*, 7 (October 1958), 104-107.
83. Caliver, Ambrose. "The National Concern for Adult Education," *School Life*, 39 (May 1957), 5-6.
84. Caliver, Ambrose. "The Problem of Adult Illiteracy," *American Teacher*, 33 (February 1949), 16-19.
85. Caliver, Ambrose, and John Holden. "Government's Concern for Adult Education," *School Life*, 39 (June 1957), 5-6.
86. "Campaign to Abolish Illiteracy," *School and Society*, 30 (December 28, 1929), 877.
87. "Campaign Against Illiteracy in New York City," *School and Society*, 43 (June 27, 1936), 868-869.
88. Cantelope, L. J. "Basic Education Resource Centers for Adults," *Clearing House*, 43 (October 1968), 121-123.
89. Carr, I. N. "Illiteracy: The Great Challenge to Southern Educators," *Southern Association Quarterly*, 8 (May 1944), 208-215.
90. Cass, A. W. "Reading Materials for Adults," *Adult Education*, 1 (October 1950), 26-31.
91. "Census Returns on Illiteracy and School Attendance," *School Review*, 39 (November 1931), 641-643.
92. Chase, F. S. "Attack on Functional Illiteracy," *Elementary School Journal*, 47 (October 1946), 69-70.
93. Chenault, P. "Correctional Institutes Helping the Functional Illiterate." *ALA Bulletin*, 58 (October 1964), 804-809.
94. Coates, R. H. "Preparing Adults for Rapid Change," *NEA Journal*, 55 (December 1966), 23-25.
95. Cooper, William J. "Purchasing Power: Education Created It," *School Life*, 17 (September 1931), 1.
96. Cortright, Richard W. "Americanization through Reading," *Education*, 84 (May 1964), 542-545.
97. Cortright, Richard W. "The First University Literacy Center," *School and Society*, 87 (April 21, 1961), 207.
98. Cortright, Richard W. "Helpful Definitions: Terms Used by Literacy Workers," *Adult Leadership*, 12 (December 1963), 184.
99. Cortright, Richard W. "Inmate Illiteracy," *Journal of Reading*, 8 (January 1965), 163-167.
100. Cortright, Richard W. "Professional Preparation in Literacy Education," *Journal of Teacher Education*, 16 (September 1965), 290-293.
101. Cortright, Richard W. "The Subject of Literacy Has Come of Age," *Reading Teacher*, 19 (October 1965), 9-13.
102. Cortright, Richard W. "They Are Learning to Read," *Adult Leadership*, 8 (June 1959), 54-56.
103. Crabtree, A. P. "War on Poverty," *Adult Leadership*, 14 (September 1965), 105-106.
104. Dale, E. "Toward a Literate World," *Education Digest*, 30 (November 1964), 32-34.
105. D'Amico, Louis A., and Lloyd S. Standlee. "Literacy Training in Prison," *Adult Education*, 4 (September 1954), 218-221.
106. "Dana W. Allen Heads Literacy Commission," *Adult Leadership*, 12 (January 1964), 209.
107. "Decrease in Illiteracy as Shown by the Census," *School and Society*, 34 (July 11, 1931), 49-50.
108. Deming, R. C. "Federal Aspects of and Responsibilities in the Reduction of Illiteracy and Training for Citizenship," *National Education Association Proceedings*, 67 (1929), 284-287.
109. Dooley, William H. "Evening Elementary Schools," *Education*, 36 (February 1916), 357-361.
110. Dorland, J. R. "Current Issues in Adult Education," *Adult Leadership*, 15 (April 1967), 349.

111. Edgerton, H. A., and M. L. Blum. "A Technique to Determine Illiteracy-Literacy Requirements of Jobs," *Personnel and Guidance Journal*, 32 (May 1954), 524-527.
112. Edwards, N. "Functional Illiteracy in the United States," *Elementary School Journal*, 54 (January 1954), 256-257.
113. "Eradication of Illiteracy in Louisiana," *School and Society*, 47 (January 8, 1938), 42.
114. "Ethical Gains Accompany Reading Gains in Adult Literacy Classes," *School and Society*, 52 (September 28, 1940), 259.
115. Evans, James C. "Adult Education for Negroes in the Armed Forces," *Journal of Negro Education*, 14 (Summer 1945), 437-442.
116. Farley, Belmont. "Alphabet and the Army," *NEA Journal*, 32 (March 1943), 77-78.
117. Farley, Belmont. "Our Lost Legions," *NEA Journal*, 31 (September 1942), 178.
118. "Federal Aid to Adult Basic Education," *School and Society*, 94 (December 10, 1966), 445.
119. Foster, R. M., and J. F. Ballard. "The Navy's Literacy Training Program," *School Life*, 36 (November 1953), 31-32.
120. Fox, Esther. "Considerations in Constructing a Basic Reading Program for Functionally Illiterate Adults," *Adult Leadership*, 13 (May 1964), 7-8.
121. "Free Classes for the Unemployed," *School and Society*, 36 (December 17, 1932), 782.
122. Gray, W. S. "Catching Up with Literacy," *National Education Association Proceedings*, 71 (1933), 280-281.
123. "The Great Undereducated," *Newsweek*, April 6, 1953, 57.
124. Greenberg, I. M. "Project 100,000: The Training of Former Rejectees," *Phi Delta Kappan*, 50 (June 1969), 570-574.
125. Gregory, F. A. "Undereducated Man," *Education Digest*, 30 (December 1964), 39-41.
126. Harris, Frances Lane. "Teaching Adults to Read with Teacher Made Materials," *Journal of Reading*, 10 (May 1967), 560-564.
127. Hershey, H. "Training Teachers for Adult Basic Education," *Adult Leadership*, 17 (June 1968), 63-65.
128. Hill, Henry H., and Ralph Cherry. "No Brand New Illiterates," *Nation's Schools*, 22 (October 1938), 29-30.
129. Hill, Robert T. "Making the People Literate," *School and Society*, 35 (August 9, 1932), 488-492.
130. Hilliard, R. M. "Massive Attack on Illiteracy: The Cook County Experience," *ALA Bulletin*, 57 (December 1963), 1034-1038.
131. "Illiteracy in California," *School and Society*, 33 (April 25, 1931), 559.
132. "Illiteracy in the United States," *School and Society*, 31 (June 14, 1930), 798.
133. "Illiteracy in the United States," *School and Society*, 36 (June 23, 1932), 107-108.
134. "Illiteracy in the U.S.," *School Life*, 45 (April 1963), 18.
135. "Institutes to be Held: Summer 1968," *Adult Leadership*, 17 (June 1968), 96.
136. Kandel, I. L. "The New Illiteracy," *School and Society*, 72 (November 25, 1950), 348.
137. Kempfer, Homer. "Illiteracy in the Americas," *School Life*, 32 (December 1949), 33-34.
138. Kempfer, Homer. "Manpower through Literacy Education," *School Life*, 34 (October 1951), 1-2.
139. Keppel, F. "Dangers of Adult Illiteracy," *School and Society*, 92 (March 7, 1964), 95.
140. Kilgore, Harley M. "Literacy and the National Welfare," *School Life*, 34 (March 1952), 90-91.
141. Kuenzli, I. R. "Federal Aid for National Defense and the General Welfare," *American Teacher*, 37 (March 1953), 4-5.
142. Lewis, J. W. "Adult Illiteracy Attacked," *Adult Leadership*, 15 (May 1966), 15-16.
143. "Literacy Training for Registrants," *Education for Victory*, 2 (November 1, 1943), 15.
144. Long, F. "Library and the Functioning Illiterate in Cleveland," *ALA Bulletin*, 60 (June 1966), 637-638.
145. Luke, R. A. "Literacy through Television," *Audiovisual Instruction*, 11 (April 1966), 260-262.
146. Luke, R. A. "Responsibility of the Teaching Profession for the Reduction of Mass Illiteracy," *Reading Teacher*, 19 (October 1965), 14-17.

147. McCormick, A. H. "Educating the Prisoner," *National Education Association Proceedings*, 71 (1933), 277-278.
148. MacDonald, Bernice. "Libraries and Literacy Activities," *Wilson Library Bulletin*, September 1965, 48-50.
149. McGrath, E. J. "Schools for Survival," *School Life*, 34 (April 1952), 106.
150. McGrath, E. J. "Selective Service Rejectees: A Challenge to Our Schools," *School Life*, 35 (December 1952), 35-36.
151. McKenny, Charles. "An Illiteracy Program," *School and Society*, 21 (February 28, 1925), 247-251.
152. Maphis, C. G. "The Veil of Ignorance," *Journal of Adult Education*, 4 (January 1932), 38-40.
153. Mason, D. E. "News for You: Newspaper for Adult New Literates," *Adult Leadership*, 13 (June 1964), 45-46.
154. "Materials for the Illiterates," *Wilson Library Bulletin*, 40 (September 1965), 51-65.
155. Maxwell, G. L. "Federal Aid for the Education of Adult Illiterates," *National Education Association Proceedings*, 80 (1942), 92.
156. Mayo, A. D. "The Significance of Illiteracy in the United States," *Education*, 19 (September 18, 1898), 30-36.
157. Minnis, Roy B. "Federal Aid for the Illiterate," *Wilson Library Bulletin*, 38 (June 1964), 844-851.
158. Mitchell, N. P. "Six Years of Adult Basic Education Legislative Activity," *Adult Leadership*, 17 (November 1968), 209-210.
159. Mitzel, M. A. "Functional Reading Word List for Adults," *Adult Education*, 16 (Winter 1966), 67-69.
160. Molz, K. "Books as Weapons," *Wilson Library Bulletin*, 38 (June 1964), 840-842.
161. Morriss, Elizabeth C. "Articulation and Adult Elementary Education," *Journal of Adult Education*, 7 (April 1935), 238-241.
162. "National Advisory Committee on Illiteracy," *School and Society*, 37 (February 25, 1933), 244.
163. Neff, M. C. "Toward Literacy in the United States," *Wilson Library Bulletin*, 39 (June 1965), 885-886.
164. Olsen, J. T. "Instructional Materials for Functionally Illiterate Adults," *Adult Leadership*, 13 (March 1965), 275-276.
165. "Our Illiterates," *Newsweek*, March 30, 1959, 66.
166. Oxley, H. W. "Illiteracy in the CCC Camps," *School and Society*, 42 (December 21, 1935), 868.
167. "Pressing Problems in American Education," *School Life*, 36 (May 1954), 120-121.
168. "Project CABEL," *Kentucky School Journal*, 47 (October 1968), 46-47.
169. Punke, H. H. "Literacy, Relief, and Adult Education in Georgia," *School and Society*, 42 (October 12, 1935), 514-517.
170. Rawlings, William M. "The Fundamental Tools of Learning," *Baltimore Bulletin of Education*, 33 (June 1956), 37-41.
171. Reece, B. Carroll. "The High Cost of Illiteracy," *School Life*, 34 (May 1952), 115-116.
172. Robinson, H. M. "Training Illiterates in the Army," *Elementary School Journal*, 52 (April 1952), 440-442.
173. Ross, Charles S. "Literacy Training in the Navy," *School and Society*, 63 (March 23, 1946), 203-204.
174. Roucek, J. S. "Role of Literacy and Illiteracy in Social Change," *International Review of Education*, 13 (1967), 483-491.
175. Russell, W. F. "Shortages in Education in the Midst of Plenty," *Teachers College Record*, 44 (November 1942), 75-83.
176. Schenz, R. F. "Meeting Community Needs through Specially Funded Programs," *Journal of Secondary Education*, 44 (May 1969), 216-219.
177. Scully, J. H., and H. J. Mahoney. "Study of Reading Ability in CCC Camps," *Education*, 61 (October 1940), 101-107.
178. Seidenfeld, M. A. "Illiteracy: Fact and Fiction," *School and Society*, 58 (October 23, 1943), 330-332.
179. Smith, Edwin H., and Marie P. Smith. "Book Selection Techniques for Adult Literacy Classes," *Florida Adult Educator*, 8 (September-October 1958), 10-12.
180. Smith, Edwin H. "Writing Literacy Materials for Adults," *Florida Adult Educator*, 9 (January-February 1959), 14-17.

181. Smoker, D. E. "Southwestern Cooperative Educational Laboratory: Adult Basic Education Project," *Adult Leadership*, 17 (June 1968), 73-74.
182. Spaulding, S. "Research on Content, Methods, and Techniques in Education for Development," *Review of Educational Research*, 38 (June 1968), 277-292.
183. Spencer, Marion D. "A Reading Center for Adults in the Public Library," *Wilson Library Bulletin*, 40 (September 1965), 78-79.
184. Stavisky, Samuel. "Ignorance Cuts Production and Defense," *Nation's Business*, 42 (July 1954), 23-24.
185. Stewart, David C. "Reading, Writing, and Television," *Harper's*, June 1959, 58-59.
186. Strang, Ruth. "Contribution of the Psychology of Reading to International Cooperation," *School and Society*, 67 (June 31, 1948), 65-68.
187. Summers, E. G. "Adult Basic Education: A New Dimension in Reading?" *Adult Leadership*, 15 (May 1966), 2-4.
188. Summers, E. G. "Materials for Adult Basic Education," *Journal of Reading*, 10 (April 1967), 457-467.
189. "Textbook Publishers Plan Conference on Literacy," *Adult Leadership*, 12 (January 1964), 208.
190. Thompson, F., Jr. "Adult Undereducation," *Adult Leadership*, 12 (June 1963), 49-50.
191. Thompson, H. "Education of American Indians," *Education Digest*, 29 (May 1964), 48-50.
192. Thompson, H. "Indian Materials Centers," *Audiovisual Instruction*, 10 (January 1965), 38-39.
193. Tyler, I. K. "Combating Illiteracy with Television," *Audiovisual Communication Review*, 13 (Fall 1965), 309-324.
194. "Unesco Plan to Cut Illiteracy," *School and Society*, 90 (November 3, 1962), 369.
195. Witty, Paul. "The Conquest of Illiteracy," *School and Society*, 62 (July 7, 1945), 1-3.
196. Witty, Paul A. "Some Suggestions for Vocabulary Development in Public Schools," *Education Administration and Supervision*, 31 (May 1945), 271-282.
197. Witty, Paul A., and W. W. Cruze. "The 3 Rs Go to War," *Progressive Education*, 20 (December 1943), 364-365.
198. Witty, Paul A., and Samuel Goldberg. "The Army's Training Program for Illiterate, Non-English Speaking, and Educationally Retarded Men," *Elementary English*, 20 (December 1943), 306-311.
199. Witty, Paul A., and Samuel Goldberg. "Evolution in Education through Army Experience," *Journal of Educational Psychology*, 35 (September 1944), 338-346.
200. Witty, Paul A., and Samuel Goldberg. "The Use of Visual Aids in the Army," *Journal of Educational Psychology*, 35 (February 1944), 82-90.
201. Witty, Paul A., and Golda Van Buskirk. "The Soldier Learns to Read," *National Parent Teacher*, 38 (February 1944), 8-10.
202. Wood, W. R. "Community Responsibility for Literacy Education," *School Life*, 34 (November 1951), 23.
203. "World Illiteracy," *School and Society*, 30 (September 28, 1929), 423-424.
204. Yearley, C. K., Jr. "The Pool of Ignorance," *Commonweal*, 71 (November 6, 1959), 175-177.
205. Youngs, M. H. "Media for Adult Basic Education," *Audiovisual Instruction*, 13 (November 1968) 993-994.

Public Documents

206. Alabama State Department of Education. Illiteracy Commission. *Report of a Special Drive Against Illiteracy among Men of Draft Age*. Montgomery, Alabama: Brown Printing, 1918.
207. Dale, Edgar. *Stories for Today*. Madison, Wisconsin: U.S. Armed Forces Institute, 1954.
208. Harding, Lowry W., and James B. Burr. *Friends in the Service*. Madison, Wisconsin: U.S. Armed Forces Institute. n.d.
209. Harding, Lowry W., and James B. Burr. *Men in the Armed Forces, A Serviceman's Reader*. Madison, Wisconsin: U.S. Armed Forces Institute, 1949.

210. Harding, Lowry W., and James B. Burr. *Passes to Pleasant Reading*. Madison, Wisconsin: U.S. Armed Forces Institute, 1949.
211. Harding, Lowry W., and James B. Burr. *Servicemen Learn to Read, Practice Books I and II*. Madison, Wisconsin: U.S. Armed Forces Institute, 1949.
212. New York State Department of Education. *Second Annual Report*. Albany: State Department of Education, 1906.
213. North Carolina Public Schools. *Adult Illiteracy in North Carolina and Plans for Its Elimination*. Raleigh: Office of State Superintendent of Public Schools, 1915.
214. South Carolina State Department of Education. Illiteracy Commission. *Report of State Supervisor of Adult Schools*, Wil Lou Gray. n. p.: n. p., 1920.
215. U.S. Congress. House. *An Act to Extend and Amend the Elementary and Secondary Education Act of 1965 and for other Purposes*. H.R. 69, 93rd Congress, August 21, 1974.
216. U.S. Congress. House. *A Bill to Make Possible Appropriate, Economical and Accessible Learning Opportunities for All Adults, both for Their Individual Fulfillment and for the Social and Economic Well Being of the Nation*. H.R. 5292, 92nd Congress, 1st session, 1971.
217. U.S. Congress. House. Committee on Education. H.R. 3923, 68th Congress, 1924.
218. U.S. Congress. House. National Advisory Committee on Adult Basic Education. *Adult Basic Education; Strengthening the Foundation of Our Democratic Society*, second annual report, 91st Congress, 1969.
219. U.S. Department of Commerce. Bureau of the Census. *Census of Population: 1950* (Volume 2), *Characteristics of the Population* (Part 1), *United States Summary*.
220. U.S. Department of Commerce. Bureau of the Census. *Census of Population: 1970* (Volume 1), *Characteristics of the Population* (Part 1), *United States Summary* (Section 1).
221. U.S. Department of Commerce. Bureau of the Census. *Census of Population: 1970* (Volume 1), *Characteristics of the Population* (Part 1), *United States Summary* (Section 2).
222. U.S. Department of Commerce. Bureau of the Census. *Education of the American Population*, John K. Folger and Charles B. Nam. 1960 Census Monograph. Washington, D. C.: Government Printing Office, 1967.
223. U.S. Department of Commerce. Bureau of the Census. "Educational Attainment and Literacy of Workers: October 1952," *Current Population Reports*. Labor Force Series P-50, No. 49. Washington, D. C.: Government Printing Office, 1953.
224. U.S. Department of Commerce. Bureau of the Census. "Educational Attainment," *Census of Population: 1970, Subject Reports*. Final Report PC (2)-5B. Washington, D. C.: Government Printing Office, 1973.
225. U.S. Department of Commerce. Bureau of the Census. "Educational Attainment in the United States: March 1973 and 1974," *Current Population Reports: Population Characteristics*. Series P-20, No. 274. Washington, D. C.: Government Printing Office, 1974.
226. U.S. Department of Commerce. Bureau of the Census. "Educational Attainment: March 1972," *Current Population Reports: Population Characteristics*. Series P-20, No. 243. Washington, D. C.: Government Printing Office, 1972.
227. U.S. Department of Commerce. Bureau of the Census. "Estimates of Illiteracy by States: 1950," *Current Population Reports*. Series P-23, No. 6. Washington, D. C.: Government Printing Office, 1959.
228. U.S. Department of Commerce. Bureau of the Census. "Estimates of Illiteracy by States: 1960," *Current Population Reports*. Series P-23, No. 8. Washington, D. C.: Government Printing Office, 1963.
229. U.S. Department of Commerce. Bureau of the Census. *Fifteenth Census of the United States, 1930: Population*, Volume 2.
230. U.S. Department of Commerce. Bureau of the Census. *Fourteenth Census of the United States Taken in the Year 1920*.
231. U.S. Department of Commerce. Bureau of the Census. *Historical Statistics of the United States, Colonial Times to 1957*. Series H 407-411. Washington, D. C.: Government Printing Office, 1960.
232. U.S. Department of Commerce. Bureau of the Census. "Illiteracy in the United States: November 1969," *Current Population Reports: Population Characteristics*. Series P-20, No. 217. Washington, D. C.: Government Printing Office, 1971.

233. U.S. Department of Commerce. Bureau of the Census. "Illiteracy in the United States: October 1947," *Current Population Reports: Population Characteristics*. Series P-20, No. 20. Washington, D. C.: Government Printing Office, 1948.

234. U.S. Department of Commerce. Bureau of the Census. "Literacy and Educational Attainment: March 1959," *Current Population Reports: Population Characteristics*. Series P-20, No. 99. Washington, D. C.: Government Printing Office, 1960.

235. U.S. Department of Commerce. Bureau of the Census. "School Enrollment and Educational Attainment for the United States: 1960," *1960 Census of Population Supplementary Reports*. PC (S1)-20. Washington, D. C.: Government Printing Office, 1962.

236. U.S. Department of Commerce. Bureau of the Census. "School Enrollment, Educational Attainment, and Illiteracy: October 1952," *Current Population Reports: Population Characteristics*. Series P-20, No. 45. Washington, D. C.: Government Printing Office, 1953.

237. U.S. Department of Commerce. Bureau of the Census. *Sixteenth Census of the United States, 1940: Population* (Volume 4), *United States Summary* (Part 2).

238. U.S. Department of Commerce. Bureau of the Census. *Thirteenth Census of the United States Taken in the Year 1910, Population* (Volume 1).

239. U.S. Department of Commerce. Bureau of the Census. *United States Census of Population 1960, United States Summary: Detailed Characteristics*. PC (1) 1 D U.S.

240. U.S. Department of Health, Education, and Welfare. Office of Education. *Adult Basic Education: A Bibliography from the Educational Materials Center*, Lois B. Watt and Sidney E. Murphy. OE 14031-41. Washington, D. C.: Government Printing Office, 1968.

241. U.S. Department of Health, Education, and Welfare, Office of Education. *Adult Education Services of State Department of Education*, John B. Holden. Washington, D. C.: Government Printing Office, 1959.

242. U.S. Department of Health, Education, and Welfare. Office of Education. *Curriculum Guide to Adult Basic Education: Beginning Level*. OE 13032. Washington, D. C.: Government Printing Office, 1966.

243. U.S. Department of Health, Education, and Welfare. Office of Education. *Curriculum Guide to Adult Basic Education: Intermediate Level*. OE 13031. Washington, D. C.: Government Printing Office, 1966.

244. U.S. Department of Health, Education, and Welfare. Office of Education. *Education of the Adult Migrant*, Edward Brice. Office of Education Bulletin No. 6. Washington, D. C.: Government Printing Office, 1961.

245. U.S. Department of Health, Education, and Welfare. Office of Education. *Fundamental Education: The What, How, Where, and Why of It*, Ambrose Caliver. Office of Education Leaflet. Washington, D. C: Government Printing Office, 1958.

246. U.S. Department of Health, Education, and Welfare. Office of Education. *Lifetime of Learning, Adult Basic Education, Community Service and Continuing Education*. OE 13034. Washington, D. C.: Government Printing Office, 1969.

247. U.S. Department of Health, Education, and Welfare. Office of Education. *Literacy and Basic Elementary Education for Adults*, Betty Arnett Ward. Office of Education Bulletin No. 19. Washington, D. C.: Government Printing Office, 1961.

248. U.S. Department of Health, Education, and Welfare. Office of Education. *Literacy Education, National Statistics, and Other Data*, Ambrose Caliver. Office of Education Circular No. 376. Washington, D. C.: Government Printing Office, 1953.

249. U.S. Department of Health, Education, and Welfare. Office of Education. Committee on Adult Basic Education. *Strengthening the Foundation of Our Democratic Society*. Washington, D. C.: Government Printing Office, 1969.

250. U.S. Department of Health, Education, and Welfare. Office of Education. Division of Adult Education. *Teacher Training Opportunities, Adult Basic Education 1970-1971*. OE 13038. Washington, D. C.: Government Printing Office.

Selected Bibliography

251. U.S. Department of Interior. Bureau of Education. *Adult Education for Foreign-Born and Native Illiterates*, Charles M. Herlihy. Bureau of Education Bulletin No. 36. Washington, D. C.: Government Printing Office, 1925.

252. U.S. Department of Interior. Bureau of Education. *Adult Illiteracy*, Winthrop Talbot. Bureau of Education Bulletin No. 35. Washington, D. C.: Government Printing Office, 1916.

253. U.S. Department of Interior. Bureau of Education. *Americanization as a War Measure*. Bureau of Education Bulletin No. 18. Washington, D. C.: Government Printing Office, 1918.

254. U.S. Department of Interior. Bureau of Education. *Americanization in the United States*, John J. Mahoney. Bureau of Education Bulletin No. 31. Washington, D. C.: Government Printing Office, 1923.

255. U.S. Department of Interior. Bureau of Education. *Child Labor*. Lessons in Community and National Life Series, Leaflet No. 24. Washington, D. C.: Government Printing Office, 1918.

256. U.S. Department of Interior. Bureau of Education. *Community Americanization*, Fred C. Butler. Bureau of Education Bulletin No. 76. Washington, D.C.: Government Printing Office, 1919.

257. U.S. Department of Interior. Bureau of Education. *Education as Encouraged by Industry*, Charles H. Judd. Lessons in Community and National Life Series, Leaflet No. 7. Washington, D. C.: Government Printing Office, 1917.

258. U.S. Department of Interior. Bureau of Education. *Education Pays the State*, Merle A. Foster. Bureau of Education Bulletin No. 33. Washington, D. C.: Government Printing Office, 1925.

259. U.S. Department of Interior. Bureau of Education. *Elementary Instruction of Adults*, Charles M. Herlihy. Bureau of Education Bulletin No. 8. Washington, D. C.: Government Printing Office, 1925.

260. U.S. Department of Interior. Bureau of Education. *Helps for Teachers of Adult Immigrants and Native Illiterates*, L. R. Alderman. Bureau of Education Bulletin No. 27. Washington, D. C.: Government Printing Office, 1928.

261. U.S. Department of Interior. Bureau of Education. *Illiteracy in the United States and an Experiment for Its Elimination*. Bureau of Education Bulletin No. 20. Washington, D. C.: Government Printing Office, 1913.

262. U.S. Department of Interior. Bureau of Education. *A Manual of Educational Legislation*. Bureau of Education Bulletin No. 4. Washington, D. C.: Government Printing Office, 1919.

263. U.S. Department of Interior. Bureau of Education. *Methods of Teaching Adult Aliens and Native Illiterates for Use in Colleges, Universities, and Normal Schools, and for Teachers of Adults*. Bureau of Education Bulletin No. 7. Washington, D. C.: Government Printing Office, 1927.

264. U.S. Department of Interior. Bureau of Education. *Problems of Adult Education in Passaic, New Jersey*. Bureau of Education Bulletin No. 4. Washington, D. C.: Government Printing Office, 1920.

265. U.S. Department of Interior. Bureau of Education. *Public Education of Adults in the Years 1924-1926*, L. R. Alderman. Bureau of Education Bulletin No. 18. Washington, D. C.: Government Printing Office, 1927.

266. U.S. Department of Interior. Bureau of Education. *Public Evening Schools for Adults*, L. R. Alderman. Bureau of Education Bulletin No. 21. Washington, D. C.: Government Printing Office, 1927.

267. U.S. Department of Interior. Bureau of Education. *State Americanization*, Fred C. Butler. Bureau of Education Bulletin No. 21. Washington, D. C.: Government Printing Office, 1919.

268. U.S. Department of Interior. Bureau of Education. *Teaching English to Aliens: A Bibliography of Textbooks, Dictionaries and Glossaries, and Aids to Librarians*, Winthrop Talbot. Bureau of Education Bulletin No. 39. Washington, D. C.: Government Printing Office, 1917.

269. U.S. Department of Interior. Bureau of Education. *Teaching English to the Foreign Born*, Henry H. Goldberger. Bureau of Education Bulletin No. 80 . Washington, D. C.: Government Printing Office, 1919.

270. U.S. Department of Interior. Bureau of Education. *Training Teachers for Americanization*, John J. Mahoney. Bureau of Education Bulletin No. 12. Washington, D. C.: Government Printing Office, 1920.

271. U.S. Department of Interior. Census Office. *Twelfth Census of the United States Taken in the Year 1900, Population* (Volume 2).

272. U.S. Department of Interior. Bureau of Education. *Biennial Survey of*

Education. 1926-1928. Office of Education Bulletin No. 16. Washington, D.C.: Government Printing Office, 1930.

273. U.S. Department of Interior. Bureau of Education. *Biennial Survey of Education, 1928-1930,* L. R. Alderman and Ellen C. Lombard. Office of Education Bulletin No. 20. Washington, D. C.: Government Printing Office, 1931.

274. U.S. Department of Interior. Bureau of Education. Vocational Division. *CCC Camp Life Readers and Workbook.* Language Usage Series 1-3. Washington, D. C.: Government Printing Office, 1939-1940.

275. U.S. Department of Interior. Bureau of Education. *Manual for Instructors in CCC Camps,* M. Reed Bass. CCC Vocational Series. Washington, D. C.: Government Printing Office, 1935.

276. U.S. Federal Security Agency. Office of Education. *Project for Adult Education of Negroes, Third Progress Report.* Office of Education Circular No. 246. Washington, D. C.: Government Printing Office, 1948.

277. U.S. Federal Security Agency. Office of Education. *Selected Approaches to Adult Education,* Homer Kempfer and Grace S. Wright. Office of Education Bulletin No. 16. Washington, D. C.: Government Printing Office, 1950.

278. U.S. Federal Security Agency. Office of Education. *Supervision of Education for Out-of-School Youth and Adults as a Foundation of State Departments of Education.* Office of Education Bulletin No. 6. Washington, D. C.: Government Printing Office, 1941.

279. Virginia. Department of Public Instruction. *Illiteracy in Virginia: Some Facts Which Cannot Be Overlooked,* E. R. Chesterman. Richmond, Virginia: Superintendent of Public Printing, 1914.

Eric Documents

280. *ABE Learning Center Guidelines.* Camden, New Jersey: Camden Adult Basic Education Learning Center, 1969. Eric, ED 051-501.

281. Adams, Kathlyn C. *Right to Read for Adults, Final Report.* Rochester, New York: Monroe County Library System, 1974. Eric, ED 044-599.

282. *Adult Basic Education, A Bibliography of Materials.* Lansing, Michigan: Michigan State Department of Education, 1969. Eric, ED 098-393.

283. *Adult Basic Education, Evaluation Report 1971.* Lincoln, Nebraska: Department of Adult and Continuing Education, University of Nebraska, 1971. Eric, ED 061-496.

284. *Adult Basic Education, Number 1.* Current Information Sources. Syracuse, New York: Syracuse University, Eric Clearinghouse on Adult Education, 1967. Eric, ED 014-024.

285. Adult Education Association of USA. *Federal Support for Adult Education: A Directory of Programs and Services.* Washington, D. C.: Adult Education Association of USA, 1966. Eric, ED 010-679.

286. *Appalachian Adult Basic Education Teacher Trainer Reading Workshop.* Morehead, Kentucky: Morehead State University, 1970. Eric, ED 054-426.

287. Baker, James P. *1970 National Institute on Instructional Television and Adult Basic Education: Final Narrative Report.* University of Maryland, College Park Conferences and Institutes Division, 1972. Eric, ED 059-468.

288. Bell, T. H. *Getting Down to Basics in Reading.* Washington, D. C., 1974. Eric, ED 096-631.

289. *Bibliography for Migrant Education Programs.* Washington, D. C.: Educational Systems, 1968. Eric, ED 030-052.

290. Brickner, Anne, and Donald R. Senter. *Learning 100 System Use with Project 100,000 Inductees, Fort Polk Training Center.* Huntington, New York: Educational Developmental Labs, 1969. Eric, ED 044-550.

291. Caldwell, Robert H. *Literacy Development Using a Programed Text and Computer Assisted Instruction.* American Education Research Association, 1974. Eric, ED 089-216.

292. Casey, Genevieve M. (Ed.). *Public Library Service to the Illiterate Adult.* Detroit, Michigan: Wayne State University, Office of Urban Library Research, 1972. Eric, ED 067-133.

293. Central California Action Associates. *Semiannual Report: August 1, 1968-January 1, 1969.* Fresno, California: Central California Action Associates, 1969. Eric, ED 045-235.

294. Clegg, Denzil O. *Adult Teaching and Learning. Heuristics of Adult Education:*

Courses of Study for Professional Preparation of Educators of Adults. Ft. Collins, Colorado: Colorado State University, 1970. Eric, ED 060-400.

295. Cole, James L. *The Application of Computer Technology to the Instruction of Undereducated Adults, Final Report.* Raleigh, North Carolina: North Carolina State University, Raleigh Adult Learning Center, 1971. Eric, ED 056-304.

296. Collings, Mary Louise (Ed.). *Programed Instruction and Computer Assisted Instruction in Adult Basic Education.* Raleigh, North Carolina: North Carolina State University, 1971. Eric, ED 051-456.

297. *Continuation of Applying the Individually Prescribed Instruction System to ABE Programs in Nevada and other Field Test Sites, Final Report.* Philadelphia: Research for Better Schools, 1971. Eric, ED 060-457.

298. Curry, Robert. *Adult Literacy: Progress and Problems.* Bethesda, Maryland: Eric Clearinghouse of Information and Evaluation on Reading, 1966. ED 012-215.

299. DeCrow, Roger (Ed.). *Adult Reading Abilities: Definitions and Measurements.* Washington, D. C.: National Reading Center Foundation, 1972. Eric, ED 068-810.

300. DeCrow, Roger (Ed.). *Adult Reading Development: An Information Awareness Service.* Washington, D. C.: National Reading Center Foundation. Eric, ED 068-808.

301. DeCrow, Roger (Ed.). *National Right to Read Partners.* Washington, D. C.: National Reading Center Foundation, 1972. Eric, ED 068-812.

302. *Demonstration, Developmental, and Research Project for Programs, Materials, Facilities, and Educational Technology for Undereducated Adults.* Morehead, Kentucky: Morehead State University, 1970. Eric, ED 054-411.

303. *Demonstration, Developmental, and Research Project for Programs, Materials, Facilities, and Educational Technology for Undereducated Adults, Ohio State Module.* Morehead, Kentucky: Morehead State University, 1970. Eric, ED 054-425.

304. *Demonstration, Developmental, and Research Project for Programs, Materials, Facilities, and Educational Technology for Undereducated Adults, Final Report.* Morehead, Kentucky: Morehead State University, 1970. Eric, ED 052-442.

305. Divita, Charles, Jr. *Adult Basic Education: A Study of Backgrounds, Characteristics, Aspirations, and Attitudes of Undergraduate Adults in West Virginia.* Huntington: West Virginia Research Coordinating Unit for Vocational Education, 1969. Eric, ED 030-789.

306. *Evaluation of the Community Based Right to Read Programs.* Berkeley, California: Pacific Training and Technical Corporation, 1974. Eric, ED 098-548.

307. *An Evaluation Study of Adult Basic Education in Maine.* Orono, Maine: University of Maine, Division of Continuing Education, 1969. Eric, ED 042-093.

308. Fay, Leo. *The Issues and the Challenge of the Right to Read,* 1969. Eric, ED 042-567.

309. Fisher, Allan H., Jr., and George Brown. *Army "New Standards" Personnel: Effect of Remedial Literacy Training on Performance in Military Service.* Alexandria, Virginia: Human Resources Research Organization, 1971. Eric, ED 056-272.

310. Friedman, Lora R., and David W. Knight. *Handbook for Teachers of Reading in Adult Basic Education.* Jackson, Mississippi: State Department of Education and University of Hattiesburg, Division of Instruction, 1971. Eric, ED 075-688.

311. Ghan, Bill, and Donald W. Mocker (Eds.). *Everyone Has the Right to Read.* Missouri State Adult Education Workshop, August 1970. Eric, ED 044-594.

312. Golub, Lester S. *A CAI Literacy Development Program for Career-Oriented Youth.* Pennsylvania State University, University Park Computer Assisted Instruction Lab, 1973. Eric, ED 079-950.

313. Griffith, William S., and William P. Kent. *Longitudinal Evaluation of the Adult Basic Education Program.* Chicago: Adult Education Research Conference, April 18, 1974. Eric, ED 092-723.

314. Hadlock, Alton. *Higher Education Administrators' Institute for Teacher Training in Adult Basic Education Workshop.* Salt Lake City: Utah University, Graduate School of Education, 1971. Eric, ED 061-495.

315. Hayes, Ann, and others. *An Investigation of Materials and Methods for the Introductory Stage of Adult Literacy Education.* Springfield, Illinois: Adult Education Council of Greater Chicago, State Office of Superintendent of Public Instruction, 1967. Eric, ED 014-629.

316. Holloway, Ruth Love. *The Right to Read: General Plan of Action for School Based Right to Read Centers.* Washington, D. C.: Department of Health, Education, and Welfare, Office of Education, 1972. Eric, ED 074-476.

317. *Home Education Livelihood Program in New Mexico for Underemployed Seasonal Agricultural Workers.* Albuquerque, New Mexico: Home Education Livelihood Program, 1965. Eric, ED 020-807.

318. *Inventory of Readiness for Literacy. Phase 1: Visual Discrimination and Select Cognitive Abilities.* Albany: New York State Department of Education, Bureau of Continuing Education Curriculum Development, 1972. Eric, ED 069-959.

319. *Inventory of Readiness for Literacy. Phase 2: Auditory Discrimination.* Albany: New York State Department of Education, Bureau of Continuing Education Curriculum Development, 1972. Eric, ED 073-355.

320. Johns, Jerry L. (Ed.). *Literacy for Diverse Learners.* Newark, Delaware: International Reading Association, 1974. Eric, ED 097-630.

321. Jones, Roland. *Library-ABE Project, Final Report.* Morehead, Kentucky: Morehead State University, Appalachian Adult Education Center, 1973. Eric, ED 096-973.

322. Keltz, Dave, and Bill Milligan. *Project to Utilize Volunteers in Eliminating Adult Illiteracy.* Washington, D. C.: Department of Health, Education, and Welfare, 1970. Eric, ED 047-237.

323. Lichtman, Marilyn. *The Development and Validation of R/EAL, An Instrument to Assess Functional Literacy.* Washington, D. C.: Catholic University of America, 1973. Eric, ED 081-811.

324. Long, Fern. *Reading Centers Project: Final Report of Cleveland Public Library.* Cleveland: Ohio Adult Education Department, 1967. Eric, ED 023-430.

325. Lowther, Barbara Doty. *The Effects of Verbal and Monetary Incentives on Reading in Adult Illite.*ates, Final Report. Naperville, Illinois: North Central College, 1973. Eric, ED 080-974.

326. MacDonald, Bernice. *Literacy Activities in Public Libraries: A Report of a Study of Services to Adult Illiterates.* Chicago: American Library Association, 1966. Eric, ED 010-855.

327. McGoff, R. M., and F. D. Harding. *A Report on Literacy Training Programs in the Armed Forces: Report MR-74-6.* Alexandria, Virginia: Air Force Human Resources Laboratory, 1974. Eric, ED 096-536.

328. McKee, John, and others. *Improving the Reading Level of Disadvantaged Adults.* Elmore, Alabama: Rehabilitation Research Foundation, 1967. Eric, ED 015-117.

329. Maurer, Wayne F. *Adult Education for Migrant and Seasonal Farm Workers.* Naples, Florida: Collier County Board of Public Instruction, 1967. Eric, ED 016-539.

330. Murphy, David R. *Report on the Hartford State Jail Pilot Rehabilitation Project 1965-1966.* Hartford: Connecticut State Department of Education, 1966. Eric, ED 019-589.

331. *National Adult Basic Education Teacher Training Program for Summer 1966.* Silver Spring, Maryland: National University Extension Association, 1966. Eric, ED 022-996.

332. Nave, Wallace K. *Adult Basic Education Teacher Trainers: Their Characteristics, Attitudes, and Values.* Raleigh: North Carolina State University, School of Education, 1969. Eric, ED 051-457.

333. Nicholson, Eunice, and Wayne Otto. *A Study of Dropouts from Adult Literacy Programs.* Educational Research Information Center, 1966. Eric, ED 010-753.

334. Northcutt, Norvell. "Functional Literacy for Adults," in Duane Nielsen and Howard Hjelm (Eds.). *Reading and Career Education.* Newark, Delaware: International Reading Association, 1975. Eric, ED 091-672.

335. Otto, Wayne, and David Ford. *Basic Literacy Programs for Adults: A National Survey.* Madison, Wisconsin: University of Wisconsin Research and Development Center for Learning and Reeducation, 1966. Eric, ED 011- 821.

336. Parke, Margaret. *Toward a Technological Breakthrough to Literacy.* Brooklyn, New York: Brooklyn College, 1970. Eric, ED 046-620.

337. Pennock, Theodore, and G. W. Taylor. *Summary of Accomplishments and Disappointments, Tuskegee Institute OEO Seasonally Employed Agricultural Workers Educational Project.* Tuskegee, Alabama: Tuskegee Institute, 1967. Eric, ED 018-752.
338. *Project Homebound: Final Report.* Butte, Montana: Butte Vocational-Technical Center, 1971. Eric, ED 051-479.
339. Rakes, Thomas. *A Readability Analysis of Reading Materials Used in Adult Basic Education.* Memphis, Tennessee: Memphis State University Reading Center, 1972. Eric, ED 067-627.
340. Resnick, Lauren B., and Betty Robinson. *Motivational Aspects of the Literacy Problem.* Pittsburgh, Pennsylvania: Pittsburgh University, Learning Research and Development Center, 1974. Eric, ED 099-799.
341. *Right to Read: Education Briefing Paper.* Washington, D. C.: Department of Health, Education, and Welfare, 1974. Eric, ED 096-632.
342. Rosen, Pamela. *Test of Basic Learning for Adults: An Annotated Bibliography.* Princeton, New Jersey: Eric Clearinghouse on Tests, Measurement and Evaluation, 1971. Eric, ED 058-274.
343. Rowan, Richard L., and Herbert R. Northrup. *Educating the Employed Disadvantaged for Upgrading. A Report on Remedial Education Programs in the Paper Industry.* Philadelphia: University of Pennsylvania, 1972. Eric, ED 062-619.
344. Schnell, Thomas R. "Teaching Educationally Disadvantaged Adults to Read," in Jerry L. Johns (Ed.), *Literacy for Diverse Learners.* Newark, Delaware: International Reading Association, 1974. Eric, ED 074-453.
345. Shelby, Floyd A. *Education for Migrant Workers and Their Families.* Merced County, California: Merced County Schools, 1966. Eric, ED 014-354.
346. Smith, Edwin H., Wanda D. Cook, and Weldon G. Bradtmueller. *Techniques for Teaching Remedial Cases.* Tallahassee, Florida:. Florida State Department of Education, 1966. Eric, ED 019-601.
347. Smith, Edwin H., and others. *Specific Techniques for Teaching Reading.* Tallahassee, Florida: Florida State Department of Education, 1965. Eric, ED 019-599.
348. Smith, Edwin H., and others. *A Revised Annotated Bibliography of Instructional Literacy Material for Adult Basic Education.* Tallahassee, Florida: Florida State Department of Education, 1966. Eric, ED 010-858.
349. Sourifman, Vivian M. (Ed.). *Guidelines for ABE Learning Centers.* Trenton, New Jersey: New Jersey State Department of Education, Office of Continuing Education, 1970. Eric, ED 060-398.
350. Spache, George. "The Research and Development Program on Reading," *Twentieth Yearbook of the National Reading Conference.* Milwaukee, Wisconsin: Marquette University Center for Reading Services, 1970. Eric, ED 050-892.
351. Spear, George E., et al. *Adult Basic Education National Teacher Training Study Part I: Review of the Literature.* Kansas City, Missouri: Missouri University, 1972. Eric, ED 065-787.
352. Stauffer, John. *A Descriptive Study of a National Volunteer Literacy Program.* Chicago: Adult Education Research Conference, 1974. Eric, ED 092-749.
353. Stein, Annette S. *Analysis of Word Frequencies in the Spoken Language of Adult Black Illiterates.* Buffalo, New York: State University of New York, Department of Elementary and Remedial Education, 1972. Eric, ED 075-716.
354. Steuart, Calvert. *An Evaluation of the Educational Effectiveness of Selected ABE Materials.* Madison, Wisconsin: Wisconsin State Board of Vocational, Technical, and Adult Education, 1968. Eric, ED 042-108.
355. Sticht, Thomas G., and others. *HumRRO's Literacy Research for the U. S. Army: Developing Functional Literacy Training.* Alexandria, Virginia: Human Resources Research Organization, 1973. Eric, ED 091-596.
356. Sticht, Thomas G., and others. *HumRRO's Literacy Research for the U. S. Army: Progress and Prospects.* Alexandria, Virginia: Human Resources Research Organization, 1973. Eric, ED 073-369.
357. *Student Taught Adult Basic Literacy Efforts, Final Report.* Kentucky: Berea College, 1972. Eric, ED 068-796.
358. *Texas Adult Migrant Education.* Austin, Texas: Texas Education Agency, 1966. Eric, ED 015-361.
359. Thomas, Myra H. (Comp.). *Books Related to Adult Basic Education and*

Teaching English to Speakers of Other Languages. Washington, D. C.: National Center for Educational Communication, 1970. Eric, ED 043-850.

360. *Toward a Joint Attack on Functional Illiteracy,* Proceedings of the Ozark-Appalachia Conference. Fayetteville, Arkansas: Arkansas University, 1969. Eric, ED 045-268.

361. Valencia, Atilano A., and James L. Olivero. *Innovative and Dynamic Instructional Approaches in Adult Basic Education,* 1969. Eric, ED 061-471.

362. Venn, Grant, and others. *A Comprehensive Plan for Solution of the Functionally Illiterate Problem: A Report on the Present, A Plan for the Future.* Washington, D. C.: Management Technology, 1968. Eric, ED 019-603.

363. Vescolani, Mildred (Comp.). *A Basic Reading Guide for Adults.* Fayetteville, Arkansas: Arkansas University. Eric, ED 065-777.

364. Wilson, Robert M., and Marcia M. Barnes. *Survival Learning Materials.* College Park: University of Maryland, College Reading Association, 1974. Eric, ED 101-304.

365. Woolman, Myron, and Carey R. Gorden. *Literacy Training and Upward Mobility in Community Action. A Report on the Literacy Instructor Project.* Washington, D. C.: Institute of Educational Research, 1966. Eric, ED 022-108.

Tests

366. *Basic Reading Inventory.* Chicago: Scholastic Testing Service, 1966.

367. California Test Bureau. *Tests of Adult Basic Education.* Monterey, California: California Test Bureau, 1967.

368. Karlson, Bjorn, and others. *Adult Basic Learning Examination.* New York: Harcourt Brace Jovanovich, 1967.

369. Rasof, Elvin, and Neff Monroe. *Adult Basic Education Student Survey.* Chicago: Follett, 1967.

370. Smith, Edwin H., and Weldon G. Bradtmueller. *Individual Reading Placement Inventory.* Chicago: Follett, 1968.

Unpublished Materials

371. Bunger, Marianna. "A Descriptive Study of Operation Alphabet in Florida and an Evaluation of Certain Procedures Employed," unpublished doctoral dissertation, Florida State University, 1964.

372. Cass, Angelica Watson. "The Role of Television in Reaching Illiterate Adults with a Literacy Program Series," unpublished thesis, Columbia University, Teachers College, 1969.

373. Crossett, Virginia R. "Programs for Combating Adult Illiteracy in the United States," unpublished master's thesis, University of Illinois, 1964.

374. Drane, Richard Stephen. "The Effects of Participation Training on Adult Literacy Education in a Mental Hospital," unpublished doctoral dissertation, Indiana University, 1967.

Miscellaneous

375. Allen, James E., Jr. "The Right to Read Target for the 70s," address to National Association of State Boards of Education, Los Angeles, September 23, 1969.

376. Delker, Paul V., Director of the Division of Adult Education Programs, "Memorandum for Chief State School Officers," August 19, 1970.

377. Emery, Donald. "A Barnraising for Reading: How Business Can Help the Right to Read Effort," address to American Association of Publishers, Washington, D. C., April 29, 1971.

378. *Right to Read.* Newark, Delaware: International Reading Association, May 1975.

379. *Right to Read.* Newark, Delaware: International Reading Association, July 1975.

380. *Right to Read.* Newark, Delaware: International Reading Association, September 1975.

381. *Right to Read.* Newark, Delaware: International Reading Association, November 1975.

382. *Right to Read.* Newark, Delaware: International Reading Association, January 1976.
383. *Springfield Union.* "Ten Year Program Mapped in Drive Against Illiteracy," September 24, 1969.